D1269901

Quantum Soul Clearing

Healing the Scars Life Leaves on the Soul

Michelle Manning-Kogler

BALBOA.
PRESS

A DIVISION OF HAY HOUSE

Balboa Press books may be ordered through booksellers or by contacting:

Balboa Press
A Division of Hay House
1663 Liberty Drive
Bloomington, IN 47403
www.balboapress.com
1-(877) 407-4847

Because of the dynamic nature of the Internet, any web addresses or links contained in this book may have changed since publication and may no longer be valid. The views expressed in this work are solely those of the author and do not necessarily reflect the views of the publisher, and the publisher hereby disclaims any responsibility for them.

ISBN: 978-1-4525-4829-6 (sc)
ISBN: 978-1-4525-4827-2 (hc)
ISBN: 978-1-4525-4828-9 (e)
Library of Congress Control Number: 2012904372

The author of this book does not dispense medical advice or prescribe the use of any technique as a form of treatment for physical, emotional, or medical problems without the advice of a physician, either directly or indirectly. The intent of the author is only to offer information of a general nature to help you in your quest for emotional and spiritual well-being. In the event you use any of the information in this book for yourself, which is your constitutional right, the author and the publisher assume no responsibility for your actions.

Any people depicted in stock imagery provided by Thinkstock are models, and such images are being used for illustrative purposes only. Certain stock imagery © Thinkstock.

Printed in the United States of America

Balboa Press rev. date: 11/07/2012

This Book is Dedicated to
Caleb, Madison, Olivia, Jaymee, Davin, and DJ

MICHELLE MANNING-KOGLER is Spiritual Soul Healer, Medical Intuitive, Spiritual Life Coach, and Co-Host of *The Quantum Magic Hour* on Awakened Radio.

She is the author of, *Quantum Soul Clearing - Healing the Scars Life Leaves on the Soul*, and Founder of the *Quantum Soul Clearing Process*. She is a contributing author of *Pearls of Wisdom: 30 Inspirational Ideas to Live Your Best Life Now*, with Jack Canfield, Marci Shimoff, Chris and Janet Atwood, et al. She is also a featured contributor in her third book, *Ready, Aim, Captivate,* with Deepak Chopra, Jim Stovall, Ran Zilca, Suzi Pomerantz, Dan Janal and other international thought leaders.

Michelle is the force behind the *Universal Explosion of Joy and Transformation Movement.* Her audacious vision is to positively impact and change the lives of a billion people.

Michelle has been in the energy medicine and alternative healing field for over 25 years. Her approach to healing is multi-faceted and "wholistic," integrating mind, body and spirit for optimal wellness.

Michelle's wellness practice, Infinite Potentials Health and Wellness, serves people throughout the world. Her innate, unique, intuitive and psychic abilities, education and training, allow her to deeply explore and understand her clients' individual challenges. She facilitates her clients as they focus on strengthening the emotional, mental, physical and spiritual aspects of their life in order to create and maintain radiant, vibrant, health and vitality.

You can find out more about Michelle at
www.MichelleManningKogler.com

TABLE OF CONTENTS

INTRODUCTION

Congratulations! If you are reading this book, you are ready to transform your life and move into mastery and abundance in everything you do and experience. Get ready, because it's going to be a fun, exhilarating ride. Before you know it, your life is going to change dramatically for the better! By using the tools in this book, you will begin to experience enormous changes in your life in a very short period of time.

Right now, we are at a unique point in the history of man-kind. Never before in recorded history have we had the technologies that are being developed every day. New scientific discoveries in every branch of science are expanding our awareness of ourselves, our world and our universe. The amount of information available to us is expanding exponentially, to the point that many of us are on complete information overload. Additionally, most—if not all—of the systems we have relied upon to remain constant are beginning to fail us. Our world economies, our banking systems, our schools, our governments, and even some of our religious systems are beginning to crumble. Natural and man-made disasters are being reported from around the world. All of this impacts profoundly impacts us every day. It feels like we are being bombarded from all sides.

As our outer world is changing and often negatively impacting us, our inner selves are also being affected. As local, regional and national events impact us individually and as a collective, we often find ourselves feeling fearful, overwhelmed, and unable to understand or cope with the changes.

On the surface, this looks and feels awful, but it is actually a gift. These seeming negative events are bringing to our conscious awareness our deepest fears and limiting beliefs so that we can heal them and begin to create a different reality and paradigm for ourselves, our families and, ultimately our world.

For example, in the last few years, hundreds of thousands of people lost their jobs as the economy plummeted. When we lose a job, we are forced to look at our spending habits and ask ourselves what is most important in our lives. Losing the ability to bring home an income brings up feelings of fear, self-worth, security issues, and other unresolved emotional baggage that needs to be addressed in order to heal and create a more fulfilling life for ourselves. Ultimately, this event may help us realize that what we've been doing for a living has not been truly fulfilling our life's purpose.

But what do you do with all those feelings? How do you cope when it feels like you just cannot catch a break? How do you turn things around when you feel so overwhelmed you don't know what to do next? What can you do to not feel hopeless and helpless, when you are faced with ever increasing challenges?

I've written this book to share with you a Spiritual technology I've developed that can help you more easily work through the emotional and energetic triggers that rob you of your peace of mind and leave you feeling hopeless, fearful of the future. This spiritual technology is one that I use with all my clients, and have seen phenomenal transformations occur in very short periods of time.

It is a technology that I've personally used to help me heal the emotional and energetic triggers that were at the root of the rheumatoid arthritis I was diagnosed with in 1986. It is one of the tools I've used to change my life from being bed-ridden and on disability, to being mobile and living my life on my terms. It's how I went from feeling helpless and victimized to being empowered. I am using this Spiritual technology to help others change their lives, too. If I can do it, so can you!

I highly recommend that you start a journal to document where you are at this very moment in your life. You'll want to track your progress and the changes that occur over the course of the next few days, weeks and months, as you begin the journey of your personal transformation. You will be astonished at how easily and quickly you are able to release the energetic chains that bind you, and to make lasting changes that will transform your life and help you align with and manifest your greatest dreams and desires.

I don't know exactly how this book got into your hands, but because you now have it, I know you are ready to make huge changes in your life. This book will give you the tools to transform your life, if you're ready to get rid of all the old "baggage" that has been holding you back. You may be frustrated with the status quo. You may be sick and tired of being sick and tired. You may be very successful in what you've been doing for a living, but your personal life feels empty or chaotic. You may still be grappling with the hurts and abuses you may have suffered during your childhood. Or you may not even know what's wrong, specifically. You just know that something vital is missing and, once you find "it," everything will be better, sweeter, and you'll feel more vibrantly alive than ever before.

No matter what kind of challenge you may be facing, there is always a way to heal and transform your life. The key is in the emotions you are feeling and your unconscious beliefs that trigger those feelings.

The steps are simple and specific. Anyone can do them—even small children.

Whatever it is that you are struggling with or working through, this book, and the tools in it, can help you. That might sound too good to be true, but if you do the exercises in this book and systematically walk through the process, you will quickly find out how much better you can feel.

Are you ready? Grab your journal and let's get started!

Chapter 1

What Do You REALLY Want?

So what would you like to create for yourself? Would you like to create a magnificent life filled with supportive, loving, connected relationships? Would you like to find your "soul-mate" and live happily ever after? Would you like to earn more money than you know what to do with? Do you long to really live your highest potentials in life? Do you hunger to have passion and purpose in your life? Then you've definitely come to the right place! This book will help clear the way for you and then help create exactly what you DO want.

GETTING STARTED EXERCISE—PART ONE

I want you to stop reading right now and find yourself a notebook and pen—or open a new word document on your computer. Begin writing down everything you don't like about your life. For example, "I don't like that I feel lonely and lost." Or, "I hate that I don't have enough money to pay my bills." Or, "I hate that I can't lose this excess weight!" Whatever it is that you don't like, write it down. Leave room between sentences so that you can go back and write more specifically about your feelings about these first statements. Just continue to write until you've identified everything that you really don't like about yourself, your life, your job, your family, your relationships, etc. Write until you can't think of anything else you don't like. Don't organize anything—just begin purging the negativity out of yourself and put it onto paper. Take as much time as you need and be as thorough as possible.

This exercise may feel a little scary. What I've found over the years of working with clients who do this exercise, is that writing down all the negative stuff tends to bring up *all* the negative feelings and fears that we think we've successfully tamped down inside ourselves. This process may make you feel raw, angry, and vulnerable. It can be a very painful process. But the more vulnerable and honest you are with yourself, the quicker and easier it is to heal your past. The good news is that you don't have to *stay* in the pain much longer. Relief is on its way to you

The next step in this exercise is to go back to the statements you just wrote, and write down how each of those negative situations makes you feel inside. "I feel hopeless and helpless when I don't have enough money to pay my bills. It makes me feel like a loser." Or "I feel like no one loves me because I can't maintain a healthy relationship with anyone." Or, "How will I ever find someone who will love me if I'm fat?" Just keep pouring out these feelings about what you don't like. Sometimes, you'll even find yourself repeating someone else's statements about you. For example, you may hear a parent's voice telling you "You are worthless," or a childhood bully who taunted you for being fat. When and if that happens, write down the exact statement that was used, or that you heard, and the feelings that those words ignited within you, because that is something specific to work through.

Again, take as much time as you need. There is enormous value in digging deep and identifying these feelings, even if it brings up a great deal of pain. Remember, you won't have to stay in the pain for much longer, because we'll be clearing those negative emotions out in Chapter 4. If you are willing to do this exercise fully, you will finally be free of the past. Can you imagine how valuable that will be?

The third step is to then go back to the statements you initially wrote, and write what you do to deal with those feelings. For example, "When I don't have enough money to pay my bills, I feel sick inside and that makes me want to drink." Or, "When I don't have enough money to pay my bills, I quit answering the phone and go into hiding so I don't have to deal with anything." Or, "When I feel lonely inside, I like to go out and dance (or drink, or party), hoping I'll find my soul-mate." Or, "When I feel empty inside, I begin to eat to make myself feel better."

These "don't like" statements will be the basis of your working list that you will begin clearing later in this book. So be sure to be as brutally honest and exacting as you can possibly be. It will pay dividends later on. Just keep writing until there's nothing left to write. Again, this exercise may make you feel raw and vulnerable, but it is necessary in order to clearly identify what you do want. Just hang on. I promise you it will get much better!

As a note, when regarding clearing out old stuff (especially in regards to relationships), it is important to identify as clearly as possible what you are feeling now and what you were feeling at the time, in order to download the most optimal positive replacement frequencies.

Often, in the past, what we were really feeling is masked by anger. Anger is a secondary emotion and is a cover-up for hurt feelings, fear, feeling judged, feeling mistreated, devalued, or betrayed. There are literally thousands of negative emotions that anger can mask.

There is a part of our brain called The Reptilian Brain that immediately helps us switch from feeling the vulnerable, painful feelings into the feeling of anger or fear. Anger is a more powerful feeling than vulnerability and makes us feel strong so that we have the resources to fight back when placed in dangerous situations. It is an automatic survival response and is hard-wired into every human.

Anger is fueled by adrenaline which creates a powerful flood of chemicals within our bodies, called neurotransmitters, that are immediately taken into the cell's receptor sites of our muscles and tissues. They give us extra strength and feelings of power. These neurotransmitters profoundly impact the brain and internal organs, by shutting down our ability to digest food and controlling which areas of the body receive greater supplies of blood flow. These neurotransmitters are so powerful, that we can actually become addicted to them—just like cocaine or heroin.

If we are continually placed in situations where we don't feel good or powerful, or when we are feeling mistreated, devalued or betrayed, we get stuck in the loop of anger/vulnerability/ anger/vulnerability. This pattern becomes a negative emotional loop that eventually becomes habitual and gets pushed to the back of the mind as a "normal" part of life, because there doesn't seem to be a resolution to the problem. It then plays in the background and begins programming our minds and the cells of our bodies negatively. It even begins to impact us in other unpleasant ways, such as depression or anxiety and physical illnesses.

As electro-magnetic beings, we are both sending out and receiving energetic signals. We are kind of like a radio that has the ability to both broadcast messages and receive in-coming signals. Once this negative programming occurs, we start emitting the frequency of these negative programs and subsequently begin attracting back to ourselves other events, people and circumstances that have the same frequencies as what we are feeling and emitting. For example, if we are emitting a broadcast frequency that says, "I'm a victim," we are going to receive a corresponding signal that says, "Perfect, here's a person or event that will help you feel more like a victim."

Until we can resolve the emotional pain and energy of the original wound, we will continue to draw to ourselves more and more of what we are energetically sending out through our internal feelings. This is the Law of Attraction at work: "Like attracts like."

However, here's the problem: Because we've so successfully pushed those negative feelings so far into the background of our subconscious minds, we aren't even *consciously* aware that those feelings are permanently transmitting the frequency that we don't want to have happen to us. The result is that we continue to draw to ourselves similar people and situations over and over again and don't understand why.

When this happens, it is an indication that you definitely have old programming running in the background that has been successfully hidden from your consciousness. The hidden gift in these negative experiences is that the patterns and resulting pain you feel are trying to bring to your **conscious** mind the awareness that there is something that needs to be resolved. Once you can successfully resolve those negative conscious and sub-conscious programs, you will no longer draw to yourself the painful experiences.

Negative programs can also be triggered by a song, a smell, a name, or other similar events. If that happens, take the opportunity to stop what you're doing and identify the feelings and emotions that have been triggered. Then do the Quantum Soul Clearing Process, to heal the old hurt and pain. It is a very powerful way to free yourself of the past. I call this the Stop, Drop and Roll awareness process. Stop what you're doing. Drop down inside to the feelings. Roll into the Quantum Soul Clearing Process.

For now, start with what you are consciously triggered by. Everyone can think of a person or event that still holds some type of negative energetic charge when thinking about that person or circumstance. See if you can precisely identify what you feel about that person or event. Write down the words or phrases that clearly describe your feelings. If you can't find a specific word for the feeling, use one as close as possible to that negative feeling. And if you just cannot identify the feeling, don't worry, you can still clear it. Chapter 7 deals with this in depth.

Sometimes people get stuck in an energetic loop of anger/vulnerability and they can't identify more than a few negative feelings. Usually the feeling is anger, rage, anxiety, fear, unhappiness, sadness or depression. It's almost like a default feeling setting. They may be aware that they feel hurt, but are consciously unaware that that "hurt feeling," is betrayal. They may not be aware that that "icky, stomach clenching feeling" is the feeling of being devalued and degraded.

It doesn't help that our English language is so deficient when it comes to words that describe feelings, either! And it doesn't help that we are generally trained away from our feelings in our cultures. There are many other languages that are much more proficient in describing the subtleties of human emotion than the English language. So in the appendix of this book I've listed many positive and negative feeling words and emotions to help you more closely identify what you might be feeling. What I found fascinating while doing the research for this book is that in regards to feelings, we have so many more descriptive words for negative feelings than there are for positive feelings! Apparently, as a people, we are much more attuned to feeling bad than we are to feeling good!

It is imperative to be aware of what we are feeling and to have a way to deal with and remove the chronic negative feelings. By not having an outlet for this negativity, we unconsciously program ourselves for chronic disease, a life-time of low-grade relationships with ourselves and others, financial lack and limitation, and the inability to live full, vibrant lives. This negativity robs each and every one of us of vitality, joy, creativity and prosperity.

Imagine what life would be like if we were able to immediately clear and remove our negative emotions and access our positive feelings. I believe we would treat ourselves and each other much more kindly and compassionately. We wouldn't age as quickly. Conflicts would be resolved almost instantly. Perhaps we would be able to fully bring our gifts and creative passions to the forefront of our lives and empower ourselves and others to live brilliantly and joyfully, powerfully sharing our purpose for being here on this planet at this time. Can you imagine what a different world this could be? Take a few minutes and envision what your life might be like if you were able to completely release the past and live fully in the present. I urge you to write down that vision now.

Getting back to our original writing exercise, stop for a moment and review everything you've written so far in this first exercise. Make sure you keep track of this information, because you're going to use it in the second part of the Quantum Soul Clearing Process when we get to Chapter 4. You may begin to more clearly see a pattern of thinking and behavior that has sabotaged your efforts to take charge and make changes in your life. But more importantly, you are now more fully in touch, consciously, with the negative thoughts, feelings, beliefs and behaviors that you can release in order to create the life you *do* want to create and live!

GETTING STARTED EXERCISE—PART TWO

Now that you've identified exactly what you do **not** want in your life, how you feel about it, and what you currently do to deal with the feelings, you are ready to start the second part of this exercise.

Find a fresh page and begin writing exactly what you **do** want. Not how you're going to obtain it or get it accomplished or who's going to bring it. Just focus on what you want your life to look like. For example, "I want to release 30 pounds and feel fit." Or, "I want to fit into a size six dress." Or, "I want enough money to pay my bills and still have money left over to play with and invest." Or, "I want to find my soul mate." Or, "I want to be happy and healthy." Be as specific as you can. Remember to leave room between these statements so that you can go back to them and add your feelings.

When you are absolutely crystal clear about what you want, it has no choice but to show up in your life—and often in bigger and better ways than you can possibly imagine right now. You might want to write that last sentence down and post it in prominent places around your home and office, to remind you to get as clear as possible about what you want to create and achieve.

When you are writing these statements, remember to define what you want to create—not what you don't want. For example: "I want to feel fit and healthy." As opposed to, "I don't want to be fat and unhealthy." The latter statement is focusing on the negative. The first one is creative, and it is a direct statement of manifestation to the Universe!

Here's another: "I easily pay all my bills each month and still have hundreds of dollars left over to play with and to save." Versus "I don't want to have to struggle each month just to get the bills paid." Keep asking yourself, "What do I **really** want?"

While it is true that you really don't want to struggle to pay the bills, what you want more is to pay them each month and still have tons of money left over to spend and save. Can you feel the difference when you say these two statements out loud? Try it and see what you feel inside. The first statement feels clear, open, honest and positive. That is the frequency that the Universe will respond to in order to help you manifest your desires.

The second one feels heavy, chaotic, negative and closed-down. The Universe will still respond to this request, too. But you'll continue to struggle to pay your bills each month and will constantly come up short. That is how the Law of Attraction works. **What you focus on intensifies**. We'll talk more about the Law of Attraction in the next chapter.

Once you have what you *do* want to create in your life written down, go back to those statements and begin identifying what having those things will feel like. So let's say you want enough money to pay the bills and have hundreds left over each month to save and to play with. Close your eyes and go inside. Feel what being able to immediately pay all your bills and having tons of money left over really feels like. Do you feel excited or happy? Do you feel free? Do you feel successful, prosperous, joyful, supported and loved? Can you even imagine such a thing? Write down all the words that having that one thing would make you feel. Keep writing and keep imaging what that feeling feels like. Feel it expand and grow as you explore it more and more.

Dream big, what could you do with that extra money each month? Write that down next and go into details. Would you save each month so that you could have a wonderful nest-egg? Would you save up for the trip of a life-time? Would you buy some things that you've wanted to buy for yourself, but couldn't? Would you donate money to charity? And in doing those things, how would you feel?

Go deep—then go even deeper still. Go into as much detail as you possibly can. This is a time for getting very clear on what you really want! Make sure you are writing down all the descriptive words you can think of that describe how you feel about these positive things. These will be useful later on as you begin clearing.

Make sure you save both of these exercises. They are going to be your working papers as we go through this book.

By going through this process, just like you are now, I've been very fortunate to be able to change my life from one of lack, illness, addiction to chaos, terrible relationships, self-doubt, and low self-esteem. That is not to say that I don't have stuff come up, that my life is perfect, or that life doesn't throw me the occasional curve-ball. Because it does.

What I do have, however, are the tools in this book. These tools help me easily identify how I feel, and then help me change my emotions in just a few minutes. When that occurs, I can make quick course corrections in my life. I have been able to create better health, more peace of mind, healthier and more loving relationships with myself and others, and I experience much greater abundance. Best of all, I've been able to show others how to make changes in their lives that help them create even better lives for themselves and their families! I know you can make those changes too—if you want to, and are willing to spend the time and effort to use the tools in this book.

Chapter 2

What is the Law of Attraction and How Does It Really Work?

The Law of Attraction simply states that "Like Attracts Like." What that means is that what you think, how you feel and what you place your attention on continues to grow. If you are continually thinking or feeling negatively toward someone or about something, other people and other things of the same or similar low-vibration frequency will be a "frequency match" to what you are thinking and feeling. That means that you will continue to get more low-vibration experiences and people that show up in your life, because they are of the same "frequency match" to what you are currently experiencing and emitting to the Universe. Remember the analogy from Chapter One of being a two-way radio—both broadcasting and receiving signals?

Conversely, if you are thinking or feeling positively, you will emit positive energy frequencies out into the world. Other positive frequency people and circumstances are attracted to you and are a "frequency match" to the signals you are sending out. They are automatically drawn to you, just like the polar ends of a magnet are drawn to each other. It can't be helped. It is an absolute Universal Law.

Let's compare two scenarios so that I can better illustrate this for you.

Think about a time when you woke up on the wrong side of the bed. Perhaps you hadn't slept well and maybe things just weren't going great in your life. You couldn't find anything to wear that felt right. You burned your breakfast. Traffic was hideous. It seemed like you hit every red-light there was and were continually cut-off for no apparent reason, which made you late for work. Then, when you get to the office, the project you were working on had one problem after another.

By the end of the day, you were exhausted! It seemed like things had just gone from bad to worse. All you wanted to do was pull your hair out, get a drink to numb the feelings, or crawl back in bed. But, no, you had a flat tire and it started to rain! Aaarrrggghhhh!!!

The world seemed to be conspiring against you to make your life miserable. The worse you felt, the more negative things seemed to happen.

Then think about a time when you felt really great about yourself. You woke up before your alarm went off, feeling rested and alert. You found the perfect outfit in your closet and when you put it on, you felt attractive and empowered. You were having a really good hair day. The sun was shining, you felt good inside, and you even had a spring in your step.

Your day went smoothly; traffic wasn't a problem. You had extra time before you had to be to work, so you decided to stop and pick up a great cup of coffee and breakfast and still had plenty of time to get to work. Score! You even found a ten or twenty dollar bill on the sidewalk that made it so your breakfast was free. It seemed like people were drawn to you and couldn't help but look at you. They smiled and were courteous. You even found a parking place right next to the door! You felt self-confident, positive and everything went smoothly at work. It was like the world was absolutely conspiring in your favor.

After work your colleagues and you decided to go out to celebrate the project that got finished ahead of schedule and under budget. What a great day!

It doesn't take much to feel the difference in energy between those two circumstances, does it? I'm sure you've experienced both types of days. I know I have! And I also know, I'd rather experience the second day far more often than I would the first one.

The thing is, we have a choice and an opportunity to change what we are feeling at any given time. I'd like to share an interesting experiment I used to do when I was first learning about the Law of Attraction that helps illustrate this.

Years ago I went to work for the local phone company. I was working in the small business division in customer service and sales. It was a very high-pressure job because it was based on performance. If we didn't meet a very specific number of sales each month we were constantly in fear of losing our jobs.

In fact, I never knew from one month to the next if I'd actually have a job the next month! Not a great work environment in which to provide great customer service! It was more about getting the sale and getting on to the next call—and customer service was almost always a casualty.

There were even quotas for the number of calls each day you were supposed to take, and the ratio of sales versus calls was tallied and used in monthly performance reviews. I hated it because I'd worked for the old Bell system when I'd graduated from high school, and knew what it was like to create a life-long connection with a customer! I felt like each person who called in deserved the highest quality of customer service and if they had a problem with their phone service and systems I felt honor-bound to make sure they were taken care of.

However, there were many co-workers in my department that didn't feel that way at all. Often a customer would "accidentally" get disconnected or was passed from department to department in an effort to not have to take service calls, because they weren't generating any sales. Low sales meant that at the end of the month you could possibly be fired. This created major conflict in the department. In fact, there were many employees that boasted about how many people had "accidentally" gotten lost! It was an awful atmosphere in which to work, and the office was highly competitive because each sale counted!

Calls were automatically sent to our phone lines, so we never knew what type of call we'd be getting. It seemed like I was always the one to get the most irate callers who had been dropped or passed around a dozen times. Understandably, they were angry and frustrated! It always made me mad that most of the time their phone problems could have been resolved in just a minute or two. But by the time they got to me they were so enraged they just wanted to throttle someone and were often screaming, shouting, or being verbally abusive.

For months I put myself through the wringer, emotionally. Feeling bad for myself and for the callers, feeling angry when I was yelled at and wanting to retaliate, but knowing I couldn't. And my personal code of conduct wouldn't let me be mean to them or hang up on them.

I was an absolute wreck! I'd go home exhausted, agitated, anxious and depressed, wondering how on earth I was going to last another day and not knowing how I could quit because I had myself and children to support. I felt trapped by the great money I was making, and at the same time I was terribly unhappy. I knew that something had to change.

After going to a seminar on the Law of Attraction, and learning that we could choose how we feel in any given moment, I decided to start playing a game with myself. I noticed that when I was the most unhappy and irritated, the angriest, most volatile customers seemed to be on the line. I decided that I would test this "Law of Attraction" thing and see what happened if I expected a different outcome. So I started intending that I would only get happy callers. I would say to myself, "I only get the happiest, best customers." I would also change the tone of my voice and put a smile on my face. Callers on the other end of the phone can actually hear when you're smiling.

I have to admit this was pretty hard to do at first—especially when I didn't feel like smiling and being cordial. But I forced myself to do it, to test the whole Law of Attraction theory.

I have to say it worked like magic! As soon as I intended that I was going to attract happy callers, changed my mental attitude, and put a smile in my voice, it completely changed my experience. Usually the next person calling in would be horrible. They'd start off being angry and yelling at me. I'd say something like, "I'm so sorry you've been transferred so many times. That has to have been very frustrating for you. You've never talked to me before. If you'll give me a chance, I'd like to help you get this problem resolved. Let me look at your account and let's get to the bottom of the problem right now."

The funny thing was, while it kept them from yelling at me, it actually changed *me*. Within minutes I was no longer angry, anxious and frustrated either. I no longer had to pretend I was happy and sincere or force myself to smile. In fact, other office members would hear me laughing and joking with my callers and wonder what on earth was happening in my part of the office!

Even more interesting, was that while the length of my calls were often two the three times longer than everyone else's I was selling more products and services than most of the other employees! My managers just couldn't figure it out.

But the biggest bonus for me was that for the rest of the day, I only got positive callers on my line. They may have had customer service issues, but more often than not, I got very pleasant, happy callers that wanted to know more about small business solutions to their communication needs.

What I learned from this was profound. I realized that I was actually influencing and changing my reality by how I was thinking, feeling and behaving. When I came from a place of service and positive attitude, I actually got more accomplished and met my goals easily. Plus I was much happier and relaxed, and I actually enjoyed my job!

So what is the common denominator in all of these experiences? **It is our thoughts, feelings and beliefs.**

Both the good news and the bad news is that most of us have a vast mix of both positive and negative thoughts and feelings that we experience throughout the day. Because we are mostly unaware of everything we think and feel (unless it is a strong reaction to something), we are unconsciously using the Law of Attraction, and get mixed results in our lives.

In fact, research shows that 96-98 percent of everything we do in our lives is run by subconsciously held beliefs and programs! **98 PERCENT!!** Only two to four percent of our actions are motivated by our *consciously* held thoughts and beliefs! When we cannot release the pain, or are *unconsciously* holding on to, grief, sadness, loneliness, heartache or any other negative emotion, we set up an energetic field that brings more of what we *don't* want into our lives—and we're not even aware of what we're doing! This unconscious programming is even the foundation for many of our addiction issues. Science is also beginning to prove that those negative thoughts, feelings and beliefs, over time, begin to change how the cells of our bodies work, and that "dis-ease" we feel when we are unhappy, creates the disease states that eventually become medical conditions.

In the back of this book there is a list of suggested reading materials to help you understand the scientific, spiritual, and philosophical basis for how this Universal Law actually works and impacts our lives. I'll be talking about a few of these books in this chapter, but there are hundreds of books on this topic—and more being created every day.

Let's look at what happens on an energetic level when you have negative thoughts, feelings and beliefs.

In his book, *"Power vs Force,"* author David Hawkins has brilliantly calibrated the frequencies of different thoughts and feelings. His book is based on over 20 years of research regarding kinesiology (commonly known as muscle testing). He has tested hundreds of thousands of people from every race, religion, and continent in the world. His research was extensive and the compiled data has an error factor of less than .001%! That is impressive, to say the least! His research led him to develop a scale of consciousness that ranges from 1 to 1,000. Hawkins' findings show that those energies that calibrate under 200 are actually life draining, and energies calibrating between 200 and 1,000 are life supporting, enhancing and regenerative.

In his Map of Consciousness, Dr. Hawkins explains how destructive thoughts and feelings are measured and calibrated. The frequency of "shame" is at the very bottom of the scale. The emotion is humiliation. In this frequency of shame, a person may feel that God despises them. They often think of their lives as absolutely miserable, or that they are a miserable human being who many not deserve to live and must be eliminated—which is the result or process of resolving the shame. Can you see how this cycle would impact your emotional, mental, physical and spiritual health and well-being?

What this means is that a person who is experiencing "shame" is calibrating at a level well below the break-even point of 200. That means that the feeling of shame is causing an energetic drop in the physical body and its energy fields. If it is felt long enough, it will negatively impact the physical and cellular structures of the body.

At the top of the scale, between the calibrated frequencies of 700-1000, is the level of Enlightenment. It is at this level that a person views himself as one with All that Is. The emotion is one of "ineffable" (Meaning too great of extreme to be expressed of described in words: ineffable beauty, or too sacred to be spoken.) and the process is that of Pure Consciousness.

In his book, Hawkins states that many of our world teachers and prophets, such as Jesus, Buddha, Krishna, Mohamed, and Ghandi, to name a few, calibrated at the 700-1,000 level. Those enlightened teachers who attained these high frequency calibrations have transformed the world. Their lives are representative of Divinity. Because of their high-frequency energy fields and attractor patterns, they have powerfully impacted humanity.

Hawkins posits that one person who calibrates at the highest levels of consciousness has a positive frequency impact on millions of people, helping to uplift the masses and raise their consciousness levels. That one person has such a powerful impact, that they counter-balance the effects of the negative energies of tens of millions of people.

I agree with Hawkins, that these teachers and prophets have, indeed, changed our world for the better with their teachings. I also believe that *each* of us is capable of achieving the same greatness. In fact, I believe that that greatness is inherent within each of us, and that we are born with it. However, through social programming and life events, we are energetically trained away from that high-vibration level of existence, and our connection and power are drained away, as well.

In order to thrive and flourish in our lives we must be calibrating well above the 200 "break even" point. That is why I've written this book—to help show you a way to change the negative frequencies of your mind, body and spirit and regain your health, happiness and direct connection with God/Source.

The good news is the Quantum Soul Clearing Process can help you change your personal energy field frequency from a lower calibration to a higher calibration by eliminating the low-level feelings and the frequencies they emit. As you do that, you will begin to experience much more positive life experiences! Who doesn't want that?

Many people live wonderful, productive lives between the ranges of 250 and 500 on Dr. Hawkins' scale. However, I have found that most of the people I meet are no longer willing to settle for lives of quiet desperation, mediocrity—or even a "good life." They are striving for conscious, fulfilling, self-realized, evolved, and self-empowered lives. They want to be *exceptional* in the work that they do and the lives they live. They strive to change their thoughts and feelings in order to realize their hopes and dreams; to make their lives richer and fuller; to create opportunities for greater success and personal satisfaction. They want to soar and experience all the very best that life has to offer! They want to experience the transcendence and oneness with the Divine.

I urge you to read *Power vs Force*. It is a powerful look into the scientific basis for the Law of Attraction and into the hidden determinants of human behavior. As you read and study the Map of Consciousness in the book, see if you can honestly identify both the positive and negative feelings and emotions you might be feeling. This will give you a general idea of where you are currently at, energetically, and give you an idea of what you might want to begin to work on to change your life. The information is very valuable and will help you gain a broader perspective of your personal life, as well as how society is impacted by the thoughts, feelings and beliefs we hold as individuals.

Just a few years ago, the very popular movie and book, *The Secret,* written by Rhonda Byrne, became one of the most well-known Law of Attraction resources. In *The Secret,* people were taught that the universe is governed by a natural law called the law of attraction, which works by attracting into a person's life the experiences, situations, events, and people that match the frequency of the person's thoughts and feelings. A person's thoughts and emotions were the key to creating attractor patterns in the collective field of consciousness to create better lives for themselves. If a person were thinking negative thoughts, negative events were attracted and, conversely, if a person thinks positive thoughts, positive events were the result.

The book was based on the principles set forth in Wallace Wattles' 1910 book, *The Science of Getting Rich,* and Napolean Hill's classic, *Think and Grow Rich.*

It quickly became a cultural phenomenon, as it suggested that its teachings had its roots in ancient "secret" writings used by spiritual initiates, heads of commerce, and powerful government figures throughout the ages. It was a brilliant marketing success. And it taught some of the basic principles of the Law of Attraction, helping people open their minds to new possibilities.

As this information swept the world, however, many people believed that simply *thinking* positive thoughts without taking any positive actions would get them everything they desired—that all a person had to do was think happy thoughts and everything would be transformed and life became easy. What most people didn't understand was that their *unconscious* thoughts, beliefs and *feelings* were impacting them more profoundly than their conscious, happy, positive thoughts. *The Secret* was a great introduction to the Law of Attraction, and it impacted millions of people. Unfortunately, many people became disillusioned, and began to believe that the Law of Attraction simply didn't work.

The truth is that The Law of Attraction does work—it gives us *exactly* what we *truly* believe and feel! It doesn't bend to the will of the conscious mind for very long, because the unconscious and subconscious minds, and the feelings that are created by the real beliefs held there, are what the Law of Attraction reacts to. They are the "engine and fuel" that runs the "machine" of the Law of Attraction. Identifying what our *real* beliefs are, and the subsequent thoughts and feelings that are the result of those beliefs, that are creating and defining our experiences, is where our real work begins!

Another incredible resource for the Law of Attraction (and one of my personal favorites!) is Esther Hicks. She channels a Group Consciousness that calls itself Abraham. Their work is all about the Law of Attraction and how important our feelings are in relation to the attractor patterns that activate the Universe to bring us more of what we are feeling. They have written many highly informative books about the Law of Attraction. They produce many workshops and gatherings throughout the world to share their message.

If you ever have an opportunity to listen to them, I highly suggest you do. The information is always very inspiring. Their message is basically, "Reach for the next best feeling." When you are in what they term "The Vortex," a centered, joyful space of co-creativity, you can manifest all your dreams and desires.

I have often heard people ask Esther/Abraham, "If I'm feeling bad about a certain thing, how can I make myself feel good about it?" And the answer is almost always, "You can't. When you are focusing on the bad, you cannot get to the good."

They encourage people to "tune their frequencies" to a higher, more joy-filled frequency in order to magnetize the dreams and desires to themselves. One way they do this is through a process of "tuning up the vibrational scale." They show how to take a **specifically** negative thought and turn it into a *generally* negative thought; then that **generally negative** thought to a *generally positive* thought; and ultimately that **generally** positive thought to a *specifically positive* thought. It is so interesting to watch people make the shift from feeling really awful about something or someone, and as they go through that whole process, they come out the other side feeling much happier and feeling greater relief.

My personal experience with Abraham came in September of 2010. I attended a workshop in Denver. As I sat there, emerged in the energy of the gathered attendees and the flow of consciousness from Ester and Abraham, I could feel my entire body and energy field being attuned to a much higher frequency than what I'd been experiencing. I felt light and empowered and joyful. I felt as if there wasn't anything I couldn't achieve. It felt like everything within me was being aligned and charged.

Within a month of that workshop, I moved to Basalt, Colorado and opened my Infinite Potentials Health and Wellness clinic. I started writing this book and was asked to speak at many international events. My business flourished and grew to serve people throughout the world. It was like I'd grabbed hold of the tail of a comet and was racing through the Universe toward my ultimate destiny!

It is because of this experience that I know the Law of Attraction is incredibly powerful. All you have to do is get crystal clear on what you want to create, release the baggage that no longer serves you, and get out of your own way. The power of the Universe is bringing to you exactly what it is you desire and in even greater and grander ways that you can possibly imagine.

Ester and Abraham's work is wonderful and touches millions of lives. I must admit that as I have listened to the questions of, "How do I . . . ," I have often thought, "Do the Quantum Soul Clearing Process! You can get from here to there much more quickly. You'll clear the charge around that thing and you can then move on to where you want to be!"

Of course they haven't been able to use the Quantum Soul Clearing Process, because this book had not yet been written—until now!

"So what is this process," you ask? Keep reading. In the next chapter we will explore the first step in the process: Connecting to the Divine Within!

Chapter 3

Step One
Getting Ready to Work—Hook Me Up to The Universe, Please!

Most people believe they have a Spirit or Soul, residing within them, but aren't really sure of the specifics of exactly where and how that all works. Residing within each of us is what I call the "Divine Core Center Spark." This Divine Core Center is the REAL you—Who You *Really* Are: A divine, powerful, Spiritual Being. It is where you will feel the most powerful connection to your highest self, and to your soul. It is where you are connected with Source. Depending on your spiritual beliefs, please feel free to replace the word "Source" with God, Goddess, The Universe, The All That IS, or any specific word or name that you prefer. I honor ALL individual belief systems. This body of work is completely non-denominational, although it is spiritually-based.

For virtually everyone I've ever worked with, this Divine Core Center Space is located somewhere between the middle of the sternum (or breast bone) and the middle of the diaphragm (that heavy musculature just beneath the center of the rib-cage, and then deeply inside, nestled in an area just before you get to the spine. Take a deep breath and close your eyes for a moment. Focus your attention within and feel yourself drop down into your body. Find the exact center of your body, and when you do, you will find a place of quiet, of peacefulness, a feeling of centeredness and often joy. Many people report that this is the place where they feel deep feelings of love for their children or grandchildren. Others say this is where they feel intuitive confirmation when they make correct decisions.

Connecting with your Divine Core Center is the first step in the three-step Quantum Soul Clearing Process. By connecting within and accessing the *power* of the soul, you can easily and effective make the changes you desire.

There are many benefits to being able to work directly with the soul. When you connect with the soul, or your non-physical self, you have the power of the entire Universe and God at your request, helping you make changes and empowering you to transform and evolve in ways otherwise not possible. Working and communicating with the soul in this manner, allows you to actively get personal, intuitive guidance in a deeper, clearer way than ever before. Once you connect with and trust your inner guidance, your life will begin to take on a magical quality of its own!

Working with the Soul or Highest Self always feels peaceful and empowering. Many people report feeling a deep quiet, and sense of energy that may feel foreign to you at first if you are not used to being connected in that way. Initially, you may have some difficulty staying in this place of centeredness and peace for more than a few minutes at a time. That's all right. When you find that you no longer feel connected within, take a quick break, drink some water, take a deep breath, and then simply allow yourself to drop down inside yourself once again. Reconnect with that deeply peaceful, centered place and start again. Staying connected is a skill that is developed over time for most people. The more you feel connected, the more you'll want to stay connected, so it will begin to come easily and naturally for you.

It is from this connected place that you begin the second part of the Quantum Soul Clearing process. But before we get to that part, I want to take you on a little journey to expand your awareness and experience of your Divine Core Center Spark.

Make sure you've got a few minutes to do this exercise and that you won't be interrupted. Make sure you are properly hydrated by drinking at least eight ounces of clean, pure water. This allows your body's neurological and biological systems to work optimally, and will help you better maintain your focus. Get into a comfortable position, either sitting or lying down. If you can simultaneously read and do this exercise, proceed; or you can find a more detailed and expanded audio recording of this at www.QuantumSoulClearing. com/free-gift. Please feel free to share this meditation with others.

Take a moment now and close your eyes and just drop into that center space of Who You Really Are. Feel around or see what you see there. Many people report seeing a tiny blue flame, like a pilot light for a gas water heater or fireplace. Others report seeing a small orb of light. Still others "see" nothing, but *feel* a sense of warmth, or a place of belonging. Others see colors and experience a clear feeling of centeredness. Others sense or hear a subtle vibration—something that may not have words for, but that has a frequency or vibration. Take a deep, cleansing breath in and allow it to release slowly.

As you take another deep breath in, whatever you see, sense, feel or hear, allow it to begin to grow. Can you see the color or light of flame expand and become brighter and brighter as you focus on it? Can you feel the feeling of expansion or fullness? Can you feel a vibration, moving and expanding within your body as you acknowledge this

Divine Core Essence of who you truly are? This is your connection with God-Source, your Highest Self and your soul! This is that Divine Spark of God that resides in each and every one of us.

Take a deep breath in and feel this spark or flame begin to grow. Feel it begin to fill your entire body. Feel it fill your stomach and your chest, your intestines, your liver and gallbladder, your pancreas, your lungs and your heart. Feel it fill all of your internal organs and tissues. Feel this Light of who you are as it expands throughout your body, growing brighter and stronger. Feel it begin to move downwards, like a liquid love light, through your hips and buttocks; down into your thighs, your knees, your calves and shins, filling your ankles, your feet and your toes. Feel this brilliant light of who you are then continue out further, as it shoots out through the tips of your toes and the bottoms of your feet. Feel it filling all the bones, tendons, ligaments and muscles of your legs and feet, all the while growing brighter and more powerful.

Take another deep breath in and gently release it through your mouth. See this brilliant light growing even larger and more intensely as it moves upward, through the base of your spine, up your spinal cord and into your back, your rib-cage, your upper back and shoulders. Feel this powerful, brilliant light filling your chest, front and back. All the tendons, muscles and ligaments, all the nerve groups that originate in the spine are all filled with the brilliant, Divine Core Center Light, this liquid, love light, of who you really are. Feel the warmth and relaxation of this process as it gets stronger and stronger.

This light then moves through your shoulders, down your arms, into your elbows and forearms, filling your wrists, hands and fingers with this liquid light of love. Feel it as it continues to fill all the muscles, tendons and ligaments in your arms and hands, as it eases any tension and removes any blockages held there. Then feel as this light moves out through the tips of your fingers and palms of your hands.

Take another deep, centering breath in and gently release it. As this light moves upward further into your throat and neck and into your head, you can feel it filling your entire skull. You may feel this light activate the neuron centers of the brain. You may feel a sense of fullness and expansion as this Light of Who You Are fills your head with a sense of warmth and peace. The neurons feel like they are firing brighter, faster and more fully. New positive neural connections are made. Feel this light move out of your eyes, ears, mouth and nose, and through the top of the head, as it continues to grow in intensity and can no longer be contained by the skull. As this light pushes its way through the top of the head, it shoots upward and then begins to cascade down and around the entire body, where it is met by the light that can no longer be contained by the body and is being emanated outwards from all the pores. Your aura grows brighter and fuller as your experience this expansion of Light within and without.

Feel every cell, every molecule, every atom of your Being vibrate with the intensity of this Light of Who You Are! Now see if you can allow it to expand further, throughout the room you are in. You may have a sense of being fully in your body, and also being able to sense all the objects in the room in because of this expansive state you are in.

You may have a sense of falling or sinking through your chair or feeling like you are on top of the roof of your home. Yet you know you are still in your body, that you are safe and sound, and that you are in a very expanded state of being.

As this light continues to grow in brightness and intensity, it expands even further. You can feel it move outward still, filling the entire house or apartment building in which you live. As this Light continues to grow and expand, you can feel it burst out through the walls and roof of the building and flow, wave-like throughout the entire neighborhood. Just like ripples on a lake when a stone is dropped into it, this light of who you are moves, wave-like throughout your city or town, ever expanding in 360 degrees.

You notice that as you expand yourself outwards, you encounter other people and animals. You realize that as your energy touches these people, their Divine Core Center Sparks are also activated and ignited! Their entire bodies fill with the Light of Who They Are. Your hearts meet and touch, and there is a recognition of the Divine that lies within each of us in a way that you may not have experienced before. Other people may pause in their travels, knowing or sensing that something special has just happened and that they feel happier, brighter, more energized and connected. They smile and notice that they have been blessed in some way.

This Light of Who You Are continues on, ever moving outward, touching every person, every animal, every blade of grass, bush and tree. And it lights and sparks the Divine in all those with whom it comes into contact.

Feel this expanded light then begin to move exponentially faster and larger. Feel as it moves outward in ever-expanding waves of light and love—east, west, north and south. Feel as this Brilliant Light of Who You Are expands across the land, and throughout the continent. It moves across the oceans and into all continents and nations. And like a chain reaction, Divine Core Center after Divine Core Center is ignited and infused until every person, every animal, every drop of water and the very air we breathe is filled with this beautiful, intense, loving Light of Who We All Are.

And as this brilliant light fills the face of the planet, Mother Earth's Divine Core Center is ignited and the entire world begins to shine with the luster of Divinity, peace and connectedness. Feel Mother Earth's Divine Core Center frequency move up through the bottoms of your feet, into your entire body and feel the incredible connection and oneness with her and with all living Beings on this planet.

Know that we are all connected and One in Spirit. Feel any discord that may be present in parts of the world begin to dissipate and this connection and oneness with everyone and everything is completed. Feel the peace, the forgiveness, the understanding and love that happens when we connect through our Divine Core Centers. Feel the love and the blessings pouring from you to others and from all others to you. Notice how you feel and how the planet and its people are changing.

Play with this Expanded You. Feel and relish the sensation of oneness with everyone and everything on this planet. Bask in the feelings of peace, love, connectedness and oneness. Then, once you feel complete, you can begin to move this brilliant Light of Who You Are, back from around the globe, back into your country, back into your state, back into your neighborhood, back into your home, back into your room and back into your body. Once you are firmly back in your body, notice the expanded, full feeling of this Divine Core Center within you and know that you are forever changed by this process. (To download your free copy of an expanded audio of this meditation, go to www.QuantumSoulClearing.com/free-gift.

This Divine Core Center is that spark of God that resides in each and every one of us. This is the ***Real You***. This is that eternal, Spiritual Being that is the silent observer of our lives. It is the connection to Source that has access to all wisdom and knowledge in the Universe, if we but allow ourselves to connect in that space and listen for the answers. This is that "still small voice" that acknowledges our greatness and is the voice that tells us when we stray from our individual life paths.

It is from this place that we make lasting change in our lives. It is from this center of quiet power and connection that we can co-create and bring into manifestation anything we choose. This is the place to go when you meditate and visualize your goals and dreams in order to bring them fully into life. There is nothing you cannot have or do when connected within to this place of personal power and connection with God/Source.

The point of the above meditation is to get you fully and aware of, and engaged in, the first part of this healing and clearing process, which is to connect within to the Divine Core Center. Once you are connected in and centered in this space, you are ready to work! So let's get going!

CHAPTER 4

STEP TWO
THE CLEARING STATEMENTS AND
WHAT THEY MEAN, OR WHAT IS
ALL THAT GOBBLEDYGOOK??

Before we move on to the second step and the powerful process of clearing out the negative beliefs, thoughts, feelings and programs, it is always a good idea to set up a clear, grounded, sacred space within which to work. I do this by saying the following connecting-in prayer:

"Mother/Father, God/Goddess, Creator; Absolute, Ultimate, Infinite, Radiant-Golden, Quantum Source-Light and I are ONE. We work together as a unified, quantified, co-creative team. By the Power, the Authority and Divinity inherent within me, through my connections with, and Oneness as Absolute, Ultimate, Infinite, Radiant-Golden, Quantum Source-Light, please prep to work, clear and create. Please prepare, place, establish and strengthen Quantum Source-Light containment and protection fields around me and each of my loved ones; our homes, places of work, vehicles, finances, financial interests, gifts, expressions, and intellectual properties. Clear and remove all types of extra

souls and entities, dark portals, toxic streams and decaying universes, all their effects and everything they represent from in, on, around and through me and my loved ones. Clear all negative motivations, blocks and interferences, and all blocks to positive expressions, and clear all sparks, programs, issues and challenges that I (we) may be running throughout all times, places and spaces; at all levels layers and depths of my (our) being(s)."

This is *my* personal opening prayer statement. I've used it for years and I know it works. If this is uncomfortable to you, or does not fit into your personal belief system, please start your session with your own opening prayer or statement, or modify mine to make it your own. Just make sure you are firmly centered within your Divine Core Center space as you begin, since this is the place of connection with God/Source and your personal place of powerful manifestation.

This prayer sets up a sacred, clear, space from which you can work. It removes outside interferences that may be affecting you, your loved ones, and your home. It will give you an additional sense of peace and protection as you begin you clearing work. The basis of this statement is one that I was taught when I learned Spiritual Response Therapy. I've continued to use it and expand on it because I can feel all the unseen impactful "stuff" fall away. I always feel like I'm clear and ready to work on my emotional baggage after I've said it, without interference from inner or outer forces. So let's get to work!

WHAT ARE THE QUANTUM SOUL CLEARING STATEMENTS?

The Quantum Soul Clearing statements are the second step of the Quantum Soul Clearing Process. They are a set of specially encoded statements that work much like computer code to help strip out and remove negative emotional programming that limits us, and re-program the body, mind and soul with what we really want to experience in our lives.

These clearing statements were developed over a period of years and are continually evolving. They are the working part of the process, and as new discoveries occur they will change. The best way to keep current with the leading edge information is to become part of the Quantum Soul Clearing community at www.QuantumSoulClearing. com/membership. You will also discover how to make the most of this Spiritual technology through workshops, and personalized services designed to help you release unwanted emotional baggage, find new clarity in your life and free yourself to live and create the life-style you truly desire.

The full statements are listed below. I've also included a blank set of statements for you in the appendix in the back of this book for you to have and use. Just as an example, I have inserted the word "fear" in the blank spaces of the clearing statements. When you use these statements you will replace the word, "fear" with the feeling or feeling phrase of your choice. Please know that any word, any feeling, any set of words or sayings that have an emotional charge for you can be inserted in the blank. It can even be an object, a thing, an addiction, an event or a specific person that you need to clear out of your space. The applications are endless!

THE QUANTUM SOUL CLEARING STATEMENTS:

"Mother/Father, God/Goddess, Creator; Absolute, Ultimate, Infinite, Radiant-Golden, Quantum Source-Light and I are ONE. We work together as a unified, quantified, co-creative team. By the Power, the Authority and Divinity inherent within me, through my connections with, and Oneness as Absolute, Ultimate, Infinite, Radiant-Golden, Quantum Source-Light,

please prep to work, clear and create. Please prepare, place, establish and strengthen Quantum Source-Light containment and protection fields around me and each of my loved ones; our homes, places of work, vehicles, finances, financial interests, gifts, expressions, and intellectual properties. Clear and remove all types of extra souls and entities, dark portals, toxic streams and decaying universes, all their effects and everything they represent from in, on, around and through me and my loved ones. Clear all negative motivations, blocks and interferences, and all blocks to positive expressions, and clear all sparks, programs, issues and challenges that I (we) may be running throughout all times, places and spaces; at all levels layers and depths of my (our) being(s)."

"Clear ___fear___ (and everything it represents)."

"Clear ___fear___'s need (and everything it represents) to be in my body, my energy bodies, and ME, all my systems; my ego and all its systems; my mitochondria, all their generations and all their systems; all my generations and all of their systems; my proteins, environments, associations and entanglements; my personal and the collective consciousness, sub-consciousness and un-consciousness; all personal, planetary and universal core operating systems; all my interfaces and connections to all those systems; and how it's affecting me in any way, shape or form, time, place or space, at all levels, layers and depths of my Being."

"Clear MY need for ___fear___ (and everything it represents) throughout my body my energy bodies, and ME, all my systems; my ego and all its systems; my mitochondria, all their generations and all their systems; all my generations and all of their systems; my proteins, environments, associations and entanglements; my personal and the collective consciousness, sub-consciousness and un-consciousness; all personal, planetary and universal core operating systems; all my interfaces and connections to all those systems; and how it's affecting me in any way, shape or form, time, place or space, at all levels, layers and depths of my Being."

"Break resonance with ___fear___ (and everything it represents) throughout my body my energy bodies, and ME, all my systems; my ego and all its systems; my mitochondria, all their generations and all their systems; all my generations and all of their systems; my proteins, environments, associations and entanglements; my personal and the collective consciousness, sub-consciousness and un-consciousness; all personal, planetary and universal core operating systems; all my interfaces and connections to all those systems; and how it's affecting me in any way, shape or form, time, place or space, at all levels, layers and depths of my Being."

"Break and clear the habit and/or addiction of ___fear___ (and everything it represents) throughout my body my energy bodies, and ME, all my systems; my ego and all its systems; my mitochondria, all their generations and all their systems; all my generations and all of their systems; my proteins, environments, associations and entanglements; my personal and the collective consciousness, sub-consciousness and un-consciousness; all personal, planetary and universal core operating systems; all my interfaces and connections to all those systems; and how it's affecting me in any way, shape or form, time, place or space, at all levels, layers and depths of my Being."

"Please apply the highest most powerful Quantum Source Light Clearing statements that will fully and completely clear and remove ___fear___ (and everything it represents) throughout my body my energy bodies, and ME, all my systems; my ego and all its systems; my mitochondria, all their generations and all their systems; all my generations and all of their systems; my proteins, environments, associations and entanglements; my personal and the collective consciousness, sub-consciousness and un-consciousness; all personal, planetary and universal core operating systems; all my interfaces and connections to all those systems; and how it's affecting me in any way, shape or form, time, place or space, at all levels, layers and depths of my Being."

"Clear __fear__ (and everything it represents) from my body and all its systems. Final clear it now."

"Clear __fear__ (and everything it represents) from my energy bodies and all its systems. Final clear it now."

"Clear __fear__ (and everything it represents) from ME and all my systems. Final clear it now."

"Clear __fear__ (and everything it represents) from my ego and all its systems. Final clear it now."

"Clear __fear__ (and everything it represents) from my mitochondria, all their generations and all their systems. Final Clear it now."

"Clear __fear__ (and everything it represents) from all of my generations and all their systems. Final clear it now."

"Clear __fear__ (and everything it represents) from all of my proteins, environments, associations, and entanglements, all their systems, and all my interfaces and connections to all those systems. Final clear it now.

"Clear <u>fear</u> (and everything it represents) from my personal and the collective consciousness, sub-consciousness and un-consciousness, and all my interfaces and connections to all those systems. Final clear it now.

"Clear <u>fear</u> (and everything it represents) from all personal, planetary and universal core operating systems, all systems within those systems, and all my interfaces and connections to all those systems. Final clear it now.

"Then clear, transform, flash-burn, purify and sterilize <u>fear</u> (and everything it represents). Purify it back to source and/or sources; then purify source and/or sources."

"OK," you say, "That looks like a lot of gibberish. What does it all mean?"

PREPARING TO WORK

The first part of the clearing statement is that preparatory centering prayer or statement that we talked about in the previous chapter. These prayer/statements when said after connecting in to your Divine Core Center, align you with your Highest Self, your soul, and with God/Source. These are the words I personally use. Again, I suggest using them in the form they are written. However, if that feels too far-out or uncomfortable for you, or goes against your belief systems, please feel free to use your own connecting to Spirit statement. I honor your belief systems and want what works best for you. Whatever centering prayer you do use, however, please make sure you have connected *first* to your own Divine Core Center Space, and work from there.

When you make the statement, **"Clear <u>fear</u> (and everything it represents,)"** you are putting that energy or thing on notice that you are going to be working with it. You are asking your soul, your highest self, and God Source to begin working with you on this issue or problem that has been causing you grief. You are also recognizing that whatever it is that you are working on probably also has many facets to it. For example, the word "fear" may also include frequencies of anxiety, rage, helplessness, panic, or any number of other frequencies that are similar to fear that your mind may already have attached to the word. You want to get as much of the frequency of fear and everything attached to that word cleared away so that you can begin to feel better immediately.

What I have realized, as I've worked with hundreds of people over the past 10 years, is that the issues they are dealing with, and the frequencies involved with those issues, all have a life of their own. It's almost as if they've become living breathing entities in and of themselves. So getting the attention of what you are working on brings it actively into the clearing process and allows it to be fully involved.

MY BODY

When you say the words **"my body,"** you are talking about your physical body in this lifetime, this time and space this reality. This is the physical body that people see every day. It is the skin, bones, muscles, tendons, ligaments, cells and systems that make up who you are right now.

MY ENERGY BODIES

When you say the words **"my energy bodies,"** this refers to the etheric bodies and chakras. Barbara Brennan, in her book, *Hands of Light,* describes seven energy body structures. I have seen many more energy structures with my clients, but do not have specific names for them all, so we will use what is has already been described so eloquently by Ms Brennan. The intent for clearing the energy bodies is for ALL named and unnamed energy bodies to be cleared. Below is a summary of Brennan's description of the seven layers:

Etheric energy body—Is close to the physical body (up to 2 inches from the body). It is an "etheric double" of the physical body, which contains all the structures in the body and acts as a blueprint for the physical body.

Emotional energy body—Extends out from the body 1-3 inches. This is the field in which emotional energy flows. Our subjective experience is of feelings and emotions. It can be observed as bright, intense blobs of color, changing and shifting with changing emotional states.

Mental energy body—Extends 3-8 inches out from the body. This is the field in which mental energy flows. Our corresponding subjective experience is of thoughts in the form of words, sounds or images. It can be observed as a structured layer formed of yellow lines or grids

Astral energy body—Extends 1/2-1 foot from the body and is composed of amorphous blobs of color like the emotional energy body, but infused with the rose light of love.

Etheric Template energy body—This forms a template or blueprint for the etheric energy body. It is like a picture negative with space where the forms of the body would be and density where space would be.

Celestial energy body—Extends 2-2-/12 feet from the body, composed of beautiful, shimmering opalescent light. It is associated with the more "spiritual" emotional states of unconditional love and joy.

Ketheric template—extends 2-1/2-3-1/2 feet from the body. It is composed of fine threads of golden-silver light structuring a template for the inner energy bodies. Its overall shape is egg-like.

ME

When you say the word **"ME,"** you are referring to the Greater You—that Highest Self you. This is that Divine Core Energy that you connected into in the first stage of the clearing statements. The ME is the Expanded You, the Soul that inhabits not just this physical body, but is also connected with and part of God/Source/Spirit that exists in all times, places and spaces of the Universe, perhaps in multiple lifetimes, past, present, future, simultaneous and parallel existences.

ALL MY SYSTEMS

When you say the words, **"and all my systems,"** this encompasses all the body's physical systems: skeletal, nervous, respiratory, digestive, cardio-vascular, integumentary, lymphatic, muscular, endocrine and reproductive. It encompasses all the energetic systems of the body and energy bodies, such as the Chinese meridian systems, the seven major chakra systems, and the lesser chakra systems. It encompasses the systems that God/Source/Spirit uses for communication and life-giving. It encompasses any and all systems that pertain to the physical, emotional, mental and spiritual and how we use, connect with, and interact with those systems. And it includes systems that we may not even know exist yet. The intent is that all systems associated with or affecting the body be cleared.

Like it or not, we are very complex beings made up of, supported by, and involved with multiple systems. Almost everything in our world is made up of systems. Sometimes the systems are straightforward and relatively simple. Sometimes they are very complex. Sometimes those systems need a good over haul! And if we can get the garbage out of those systems (by using these healing and clearing statements) those systems can be made more efficient and less cumbersome so that they serve our lives, rather than dragging us down.

MY EGO AND ALL ITS SYSTEMS

When you say the words, **"my ego and all its systems,"** you are clearing the ego of the negative programming too. By getting the ego involved, you are training it to work with you and not against you. You are bringing it into alignment with the Greater You, so that your highest self, you as a physical body, and your ego can all work together the way it was supposed to be.

I was reading Eckhart Tolle's book, *A New Earth*, when I realized I needed to add this portion to the clearing statements. I loved that book, and enjoy all of Eckhart Tolle's teachings. As I was reading it, however, I had an experience and awareness of the ego that differed somewhat from Eckhart's. When I asked Spirit what I was seeing and feeling, I got a picture of a prism of glass, a vast, radiant orb of Pure Light, and a human body.

I was told that the vast, radiant orb of Pure Light was the soul and that the prism is the ego. The prism was designed to focus the spectrum of the soul for the body's lifetime when it incarnates. The problem with the ego, as Tolle points out, is that the ego begins to believe that it is the power. However, by trying to subjugate the ego with our will, we begin setting up a power struggle that can cause problems. When we deny the ego or try to limit it, it begins to act like a small child. It gets whiney and pouty and begins to act out and play the game of "I'll show you!" Ego is supposed to be a part of our lives. But it needs to be in balance.

By working with ego, clearing it of the negative feelings, emotions and programming that we are experiencing, and engaging it as a resource we circumvent this kind of conflict. Then we have the creative force that the ego can bring. In this way, the ego becomes one more vital piece of our whole Being that we can use to further our personal evolution, and to become more whole, centered and balanced.

MY MITOCHONDRIA

When you say, **"my mitochondria, all their generations and all their systems,"** you are working with a very specialized organism that lives in each and every cell of our bodies. Mitochondria are responsible for the Krebs cycle of cellular respiration in our bodies. They produce all the energy needed to allow our cells to reproduce and repair our bodies. They are actually their own species and not really a part of our DNA—even though they have a critical symbiotic relationship with us. They have their own DNA and genome. We get our mitochondria from our mothers (with a few exceptions). In fact, that is how researchers can trace back our origins and genealogical lines.

Without our mitochondria we would die. They live within all the cells in our bodies. In fact, some cells, like the human liver cells have 1000-2000 mitochondria per liver cell! Other cells within our bodies only have a single mitochondria. Interestingly, without us, mitochondria cannot exist. They are as dependent upon us for life as we are on them for our life.

I recently took a series of classes at Weber State University in Ogden, Utah. I was in a Bio-Medical Core class and we were talking about the Krebs Cycle of cellular respiration (Quit yawning! This really is interesting!) We were talking about mitochondria and the role they play in our bodies.

As I was sitting in class and listening to this lecture and furiously taking notes, I suddenly became aware that the group of non-physical entities that I work with had shown up as well. Whenever I do long-distance medical intuitive work, I call on these high-level Light Beings to help me. I was a little surprised, since I'd not consciously called on them and was intently listening and asking questions of the professor, fully involved in the discussion. I'd never had them just show up without my asking for their help before! It was such a strange and unique experience, because as the professor was giving the room full of students the lecture about mitochondria, my non-physical friends were also giving me, through words, pictures and vibrations, an expanded knowledge of how mitochondria work and what they really are.

The purpose of the mitochondria is to produce ATP—which is the energy needed for our individual cells to produce energy, grow, replicate and provide the overall systemic functions of the body. Because of their unique ability to produce energy, it is through the mitochondria that the soul actually seats itself into the physical cells of the body. Since the soul is pure energy, it has to have a way to anchor itself in, and it uses the citric acid, or Krebs cycle to do so. It is the mitochondria's function to do that!

My non-physical team also explained that because our mitochondria are their own separate beings, so to speak, they have their own lives, their own generations, their own set of unique awareness, and their own programs and issues. Because they are housed within us, if they are running programs, we can pick up their programs and run them, thinking that it is ours! And conversely, they may be imprinted and running our programming and passing it down to their successive generations. Because we only inherit our mitochondria from our mothers, we also are inheriting our generational programming of our mothers and our mother's mitochondria, as well.

As soon as I added the mitochondria piece to the clearing and healing statements, I noticed that many of the old programs that kept reactivating prior to adding the statements finally resolved—and stayed gone! Because the mitochondria provide the energy for the cells to replicate, by not passing on the programming, the cells were made stronger and healthier and were able to reproduce healthier, more viable new cells. This resulted in a reduction of disease symptoms in those with health problems and an increase in energy and physical vitality!

I've often wondered what my professor would have thought had he known just who was in his lecture hall that day and what additional information was being taught!

MY PROTEINS AND ENVIRONMENTS

When you say **"my proteins and environments"** this refers to all the basic building blocks that are used by the cells to build, maintain and replace the tissues in your body. Your muscles, organs, blood, and bones are all made up of different types of proteins. When you eat, your stomach uses digestive juices to break down the different foods into basic units called amino acids. These amino acids are then put together in long strings that look almost like beads on a necklace. Each of the "beads" are a different type of amino acid, and our **genes** encode the amino acids in specific sequences to make the different types of proteins. The body uses these basic strands of protein to create new cells, rebuild damaged tissues, and maintain optimal healthy functioning systems. These proteins also include all the cells within the body, and all the components within in each of the cells. There are an estimated 100 trillion cells in the human body.

This part of the clearing statements came about through my exposure to Dr. Bruce Lipton's work.

Dr. Lipton is a brilliant cell biologist who is bridging the worlds of science and spirituality. In the early 1980's he began working with quantum mechanics in relation to his work on cloning human cells. His work led to a breakthrough in the study of cell membranes. The study revealed that this outer layer of the cell was "an organic homologue of a computer chip, the cell's equivalent of a brain." What this means is that the "brain" of the cell is not the nucleus, as we've all been taught in our biology classes. Rather, the brain is the cell's outer membrane, and it acts just like a computer.

Think about this for a minute: We have trillions of cells in our bodies. Each one of those cells is a tiny computer chip that is constantly being programmed! Because we cannot separate any portion of ourselves, every thought, feeling, word, belief and experience that we have, is encoded in that cellular computer. The nucleus is the place where the cells, the genes and DNA are all replicated. So what the "cellular brain" membrane is encoded with determines what coding sequence is programmed into the cell's reproductive system.

Additionally, Dr. Lipton explains that our **environments**, and everything that is contained within them, as they are experienced by our bodies, are programming the cellular membranes! So when we are in home or work environments where there is conflict or negativity, we are programming our cells negatively. When we are in environments of peace and love, we are programming our cells positively. We are like huge sponges. Wherever we go, whatever we experience, our bodies, minds and spirits are soaking up the atmosphere and we are constantly programming ourselves from those environments.

Until recently, science has taught us that our genes were responsible for how our cells replicate. According to Dr. Lipton, and now many other scientists, we've had it *exactly backwards*. 95% of the time it is not our genes that determine who we are. It's our thoughts, feelings, beliefs, words and experiences that determine how our **genes are expressing**. In other words, those little strings of proteins are being encoded by our thoughts and feelings—and when we are thinking and feeling positively, our genes are imprinting the cellular functions with positive coding. When we're thinking and feeling negatively, they are encoding our proteins in completely different ways!

The implications of this are staggering! Take for example, the "belief" that if one of our parents had cancer, we will too. That belief itself may be what turns the genes on and off. By changing our beliefs, thoughts and feelings around an issue we may be able to determine whether the genes for cancer are turned on ("I'll get cancer.") or turned off ("I am healthy, at peace, and safe!")

There have been volumes of mind/body studies over last 30 years by scientists and medical doctors that show that cancer patients who have a strong belief in their wellness, and who practice radical forgiveness during their recovery, tend to live longer and remain healthier than those who do not. Some of those books are referenced in my resources section at the end of this book.

MY ASSOCIATIONS

This part of the clearing statements came from a psychology class I took. In the class we did an exercise that had such profound implications for me. The exercise was designed to show the class how each person's association with a string of words is completely different than anyone else's. It demonstrated how the brain remembers certain things through association. It also showed how using different word associations with people, could "change" an experience of what a person had observed or experienced. The exercise had so many implications for me and broadened my understanding of how we associate things, I knew I had to add this piece to the clearing statements.

The exercise was very simple. The professor said the word "honey." Everyone was to write down the first word that popped into their heads. Then she said the word "honey" again and the next word that came to mind was what we were to write. We went through this exercise with the word "honey" being repeated approximately twelve times. Some of the students had only a few word associations after eight or nine repetitions and began to loop back to previous words they'd written. Others could have kept the word associations for many more repetitions.

My association was: *Honey—Butter—Rich—Warm—Love—Lover—Husband—Supportive—Caring—Cherished—Loved—Belonging.*

Then the Professor had us each share our sequences with the class. Not one person's associations were even close to anyone else's! It was fascinating!

Then we did the exercise again using the same word, but were told to consciously write down a different associative word the first time. Mine went like this: *Honey—amber—beads—beautiful—necklace—insects—ewwww!—stinging—creepy—nasty—get away!* Isn't it fascinating how the mind works?

So by clearing **negative** associations between ourselves and the issue we are working on, we can begin to break looping patterns that keep us stuck in helplessness, rage, hopelessness, or any number of disempowering energies. It helps to unlock the bonds of association and free up the mind to think in different ways.

In fact, based on recent brain research, when we change our thinking, we are actually re-wiring our brains, creating new neural connections, and creating new brain cells. It literally affects the brain's plasticity and determines how we see our world!

Additionally, it also clears the negative frequencies of our personal associations with others. Our families and friends can hold energetic patterns. Our association with others and their programming can imprint us with negative beliefs and programs. Our continued association with them, helps solidify those energetic patterns within ourselves.

The same holds true of any type of association we engage in. If we associate ourselves with people, groups and societies that are positive by nature, we begin to take on more positive attributes. By clearing our associations we begin to free ourselves from possible energetic bonds in ways we have never consciously considered.

MY ENTANGLEMENTS

When you use the word **"Entanglements,"** you are clearing the "tangled web we weave," so to speak. Many times our thoughts, feelings, beliefs and relationships are like a tangled, knotted ball of yarn. It is difficult to unravel those tangled knots and find clarity.

I've often seen and felt these entanglements release and smooth out as my clients say these statements. It allows clarity and a focus that they'd not had available to them previously. To me, it feels like if you can just pull the right "thread," that tangled garbled mess will smooth itself right out.

The Entanglements piece is also relates to String Theory. String Theory is a relatively new science that has been called "The Theory of Everything." Some key features of String Theory are that everything in our universe is comprised of vibrating filaments (strings) and membranes (brains) of energy. It attempts to reconcile general relativity (gravity) with Quantum Physics. It includes concepts such as alternate dimensions, parallel universes and holographic principles.

String theory is a little difficult to describe in just a few sentences, because the theories are so far-reaching and abstract. Just knowing that the intent is to clear anything around this particular inclusive science opens up the potential to clear unseen worlds, dimensions, and possibilities that may be impacting us in ways we aren't consciously aware of yet. However, Spirit knows and Spirit is **very** efficient in getting the work accomplished for us. That is why we connect with our highest self and soul at the very beginning of the Quantum Soul Clearing Process.

THE COLLECTIVE CONSCIOUSNESS, SUB-CONSCIOUSNESS AND UN-CONSCIOUSNESS

When you say, **"My Personal and The collective consciousness, sub-consciousness and un-consciousness,"** you are talking about your own conscious mind, unconscious mind and sub-conscious mind, as well as your involvement and interfaces with the collective systems of the world. In Jungian psychology, it is described as a part of the unconscious mind, shared by a society, or all humankind. It is a product of our ancestral experiences and contains concepts as science, religion, and morality.

When you are muscle testing, for instance, you are tapping into the collective consciousness through the body's energy systems in order to gain greater awareness and perspective. The collective consciousness is a vast morphogenic field that holds everything that anyone has ever thought, felt, or experienced. It is constantly evolving as each of us evolves.

We are all a part of the universal collective consciousness, un-consciousness and sub-consciousness. Our individual consciousness, sub-consciousness and unconsciousness interfaces directly into the collective and vice-versa. It is one of the most important and least understood factors of influence within our society and our global culture.

When we clear our issues from ourselves and from the collective, we also affect the collective and everyone on the planet. By clearing our small part, we free up space for change and transformation for all of humanity. Because we are part of a whole, it is imperative that we take responsibility for what we add to or take away from the collective.

ALL PERSONAL, PLANETARY AND UNIVERSAL CORE OPERATING SYSTEMS

When you say, **"All personal, planetary and universal core operating systems,"** you are referring to the basic operating systems that run you, the planet and the universe.

Just like a computer, we all have basic operating systems that consist of programs, data, software (our beliefs, thoughts and feelings) and hardware (our cells, neurological wiring, blood vessels, etc). These core operating systems are the default programs that we rarely consciously use—in fact most of us aren't even aware that we have an operating system.

These operating systems are often inherited generationally. They can also be based on belief systems we are taught through religious, familial and secular training we receive. Often, these operating systems are set by the time we are about five years old—long before we are consciously able to identify whether those operating systems are supportive or destructive throughout our lives.

Operating systems provide structure for our lives. However rigid or relaxed these operating systems are helps determine our codes of ethics, how we conduct ourselves in business and personal relationships, how we treat ourselves and our loved ones, and how we generally run our lives.

One example of a personal operating system might go like this: "I get up in the morning. I get out of bed. I use the bathroom. I brush my teeth and wash my face or shower. I then get dressed. I make myself breakfast and go to work. I come home from work. I make my dinner. I watch 2 hours of television and go to bed." And this operating system repeats every day throughout the week. Then changes on weekends.

We don't necessarily have to think about it. It is habitual. Depending on how we are put together, any disruption from this operating system may make us feel uncomfortable or like something is missing.

If a core operating system is too rigid and structured, we may feel like we are being smothered and want to rebel. If a core operating system is too lax, we may not have good boundaries, have little or no motivation to be productive, or we may have no internal compass to help guide us forward in any way.

Planetary operating systems are those systems that really have a life of their own, yet we are intricately and intrinsically tied into them. Some of them are the banking systems, our governmental systems, the health care system, our school systems, our churches and religions, our systems of transportation, gravity, weather systems and electromagnetic systems of the planet. There are so many systems, they cannot all be listed here, and you probably are aware of some that I am not. Many of these systems were created to serve us; however, many have taken on a life or their own and may now no longer serve the people they were designed to serve. Some are man-made, some of them are innately part of the planet.

Universal core operating systems are those systems such as The Law of Attraction, The Law of Vibration, Law of Love, Law of Cause and Effect, The Law of Perpetual Transmutation, and others. These are the laws that operate the Universe and everything in it. And yet, all these laws and systems ultimately affect each and everyone one of us, whether we are consciously aware of them or not.

By clearing our negative energies and parts where we play in these systems, we take responsibility for positively changing and impacting these systems. We also enable those systems to serve us in more positive, supporting ways.

"All my interfaces and connections to all those systems," is fairly self-explanatory. It is how you interact and interface with all of the systems. Each of us has an energetic link-up to these systems. They can infuse us with energy or drain us of energy, depending on the system and if it's in alignment with our highest life purpose.

"And how it's affecting me in any way, shape or form, time, place or space, at all levels, layers and depths of my Being," acknowledges that you are or have been affected by all of the above items. This part of the statement acknowledges that you know you are a multi-dimension human being. While a part of your immense soul is infused into this body in this lifetime and dimension, you are simultaneously existing in multiple other dimensions, times, places and spaces. This concept of multi-dimensionality is being supported by the quantum sciences. What you are asking is that all of what has been said before is cleared out of every aspect of you and your multi-dimensional Being. In every life time you've ever lived.

When you make the statement, "Clear _____'s need (and everything it represents) . . ." you are clearing that frequency's need to have anything to do with you. Everything that exists has a specific frequency. People, things, thoughts, beliefs—everything exists at a certain frequency. Fear has a sharp, frenetic frequency. Love has a soothing, calming, enhancing frequency.

In my work with clients over the years, I have found that in many cases there is a contract of sorts that is made between the person experiencing a negative frequency and the frequency itself. It is like the frequency (or problem or thing) has to have a home in order to express itself and the person has an experience that triggers the feeling or frequency of that problem and there is an energetic "match" made. You run it and it runs you. By clearing the frequency's need to have you experience it, you begin breaking down that contract so that it can be removed and resolved.

When I do this first statement, I visualize and feel that thing I'm clearing begin to detach itself from every cell of my body and aspect of my life. Often I'll hear an energetic snap, like old rubber bands breaking and losing their grip on me.

When you make the statement, **"Clear MY need for _____ (and everything it represents) . . ."** You are asking that *your* energetic charge, *YOUR NEED* (positive or negative—or as a way to define or limit yourself) to have that frequency impact you in any way be resolved. You are acknowledging that you've had either a conscious or unconscious part in the interaction. You are actively choosing to release the frequency, issue or person, and that you are ready and willing to move on.

As you say the full statement, feel the frequency of what you are clearing come up from the center of you and just roll off of you like quick-silver droplets of water. Just let everything negative that you've been holding come up and out and release from you. Or feel yourself release that frequency like letting go of a helium balloon.

At the end of that statement take a moment, and take a couple of deep cleansing breaths, while you feel yourself allow the release of the energy you are holding. You can often feel your body begin to relax as you feel your side of the energetic change begin to dissolve and resolve.

The next section, "**Break resonance with** _____ (**and everything it represents**) . . . ,**"** Is breaking and clearing the energetic resonance within every aspect of you. Clients have often commented that they can feel something shatter or break up or dissolve when they go through this portion of the clearing statements. To me it feels like it shatters, disintegrates into trillions of little pieces of sand, and begins to pour out of me like grains of sand through an hour-glass.

Again, at the end of this section, take a couple of deep cleansing breaths as you feel the power of your words release and remove the frequency of what it is you are clearing.

"**Break and clear the habit and/or addiction of** _____ (**and everything it represents**) . . . ,**"** is one of the most powerful portions of the clearing statements. Often we don't realize that the energy we have been holding has become a habit or even an addiction! We have become so accustomed to having that energy as part of who we are, that we think it's just a normal way of life. We don't realize how addicted or habituated we have become to keeping that frequency in our lives. We are not conscious of the positive or negative pay-off we get from continuing to run the program or frequency. In order to be able to move on and heal we have to be able to resolve and remove old habits and addictions to thoughts, feelings, events and people that no longer serve the highest vision of who we are becoming.

At the end of this section, envision the cells of your body dislodge this frequency from the cell's receptor sites. As the frequency is removed, you might was to visualize the receptor sites no longer being an energetic or physical match to the frequency, so there's no place for it to attach into the cells of the body or brain.

"Please apply the Highest most Powerful Quantum Source Light Clearing Statements that will fully and completely clear and remove _____ **(and everything it represents) . . ."** acknowledges that God Source may have an even better and higher version of the clearing statements that may more efficiently and thoroughly clear and remove the negative issues. It is actively handing this all over to a Greater Guidance and allowing that there may be an even better way of doing it that we're not consciously aware of.

Our Souls work in the language of Light and vibrational frequency. Our earthly languages don't have the adequate words to completely encompass the essence of an issue. By asking for Quantum Source Light (or God/Source) to add His/Her clearing statements to our, we can effectively get to the absolute core of the issue and have it completely resolved.

What I have found is that at this point it is often quite beneficial to do a forgiveness statement. So far, you've gone through the body of the clearing statements and are getting ready to strip things out a piece at a time. The forgiveness statements are listed below, along with their meaning. You don't have to use the forgiveness statements; however there is great power in forgiving ourselves and others in order to move forward.

THE FORGIVENESS STATEMENT

- *I willingly forgive myself for any and all, actual or perceived, hurt or harm I may have caused myself or any others; or that any others have caused me or any others with* _____.
- *I willingly love and forgive myself.*
- *I willingly love and forgive all others.*
- *All others willingly love and forgive me.*
- *I willingly love and forgive God/Source.*
- *God/Source willingly loves and forgives me.*
- *I willingly love and forgive my Quantum Source-Light Highest Self.*
- *My Quantum Source-Light Highest Self willingly loves and forgives me.*
- *I am absolutely, ultimately, infinitely, quantumly loved and forgiven.*
- *I now willingly release all* _____ *and everything it represents, and go in peace, love, joy, harmony, abundance, health and wealth.*

Forgiveness is a misunderstood practice for most people in the world. Forgiveness is not condoning harmful behavior, nor is it allowing others—or ourselves—to continue to emotionally, mentally, physically or spiritual abuse us. Many times we must physically withdraw ourselves from situations or relationships in order to stop the abusive, painful behaviors.

Forgiveness is the willingness to define what we have perceived or experienced as harmful, and to acknowledge we may have had some type of roll in that exchange of energy at some level and not seek any type of retribution. This ultimately frees us, emotionally, mentally, spiritually and physically. (Remember we are multi-dimensional beings. This life that we are currently living is a tiny fraction of what we are actually living as a Soul-Being.)

Secondly we are also acknowledging that others have their role to play in the situation—either as the person being harmed or the person causing the harm. Forgiveness is not about blame and shame. It is about freedom.

Forgiveness is drawing that energetic line in the sand and saying, "I acknowledge that there has been some type of harm or negative engagement. I no longer want to continue in this energetic exchange. By allowing me to withdraw all my energy from you and allowing you to withdraw all your energy from me, we will then no longer have a negative interaction and we can each begin a healing process. I take back my part of this exchange. You take back your part of the exchange. God/Source takes back Its/His/Her part in this whole exchange. My Highest Self takes back it's part of the exchange. The negative charge between us is now resolved and we can free to easily go our own separate ways in peace and harmony."

When said in its entirety and with a willingness and intent to release the energetic binds that cause pain, this statement can clear and void vows, contracts, commitments, etc., that a person has made in all life-times and existences. It can help clear out generational vows (i.e., the tribal vows that perpetuate conflict between groups of peoples in war-torn areas of the world, as well as personal grievances, vendettas and vows we have made ourselves.) And it can help clear out any energies we may be holding for others, that are not ours to hold onto.

These statements allow us to take back our personal power, release victimization, and regain mastery over all aspects of our lives and existences. It energetically allows us to feel forgiveness that we may have been denied by others, causing self-punishment. The statements make/allow us to be responsible for our part in any given situation and it makes/allows others to be responsible for their own stuff, as well. By releasing perceived hurt and harm and applying forgiveness, we release the energetic hold others have had on us and that we've allow ourselves to maintain.

If we, indeed, are God/Goddess Spark—that Divine Core Spark that resides within each of us—and the whole world is our "stage," then we have the power, through our words and our intent to change the landscape of our "stage." We can find and create peace within so that we no longer attract to us the same energies, events, people, etc., that cause us continued pain.

As Masters of our lives, we have the responsibility to ourselves, our families and our communities to model peace from within, to continue to forgive ourselves and others, and lead peace-filled lives so that others can then learn how to live peacefully. The Journey begins with (and within) us, as individuals, and spreads outwards throughout the world.

WRAPPING UP

Once the forgiveness statement is completed, go back to the second part of the Quantum Soul Clearing Statements and begin the wrapping up process by going through them one by one. After each individual statement, take one or two deep cleansing breaths and feel the energy of what you are clearing completely move out of your body. There is such a feeling of lightness as each layer is stripped away, one by one!

As you say the words, "Final clear it now," remember that this is a command. This command empowers you to finally be done with the energy of the frequency you are clearing.

"Clear _____ (and everything it represents) from my body and all its systems. Final clear it now."

"Clear _____ (and everything it represents) from my energy bodies and all its systems. Final clear it now."

"Clear _____ (and everything it represents) from ME and all my systems. Final clear it now."

"Clear _____ (and everything it represents) from my ego and all its systems. Final clear it now."

"Clear _____ (and everything it represents) from my mitochondria, all their generations and all their systems. Final Clear it now."

"Clear _____ (and everything it represents) from all of my generations and all their systems. Final Clear it now."

"Clear _____ (and everything it represents) from all of my proteins, environments, associations, and entanglements, all their systems, and all my interfaces and connections to all those systems. Final clear it now.

"Clear _____ (and everything it represents) from the collective consciousness, sub-conscious and un-consciousness, all their systems, and all my interfaces and connections to all those systems. Final clear it now.

"Clear _____ (and everything it represents) from all Personal, Planetary and Universal Core Operating Systems, all systems within those systems and all my interfaces and connections to all those systems. Final clear it now.

And then the final clearing statement:

"Then clear, transform, flash-burn, purify and sterilize _____ (and everything it represents). Purify it back to Source and/or Sources; then Purify Source and/or Sources."

The intent of the last statement is that the frequency be completely removed and sent back to its origin, as if it had never happened in the first place. As a note, if you are clearing a specific person and their energy, please know that you are not eliminating them in any way. What you are doing, however, is eliminating the negative energy of that person that is affecting you. There is a difference!

People are often shocked when they physically feel the energy move throughout their bodies and leave. As you go through this process, you may experience muscle twitches or spasms. You might feel like laughing or crying. You might immediately notice that the noise (or voices) in your head is completely gone. You will usually feel buoyant, joyful and experience a profound relief that a heavy load has been lifted.

Please know that you may also feel very tired, and need food or a nap. The energy that has been expended holding negative energy and then having it released is big work, and it can cause you to feel exhausted as all your systems are re-booted and reprogrammed. It can be a big deal!

Make sure that you drink plenty of water throughout this process, to keep your body and electrical systems hydrated. That will help prevent you from feeling as tired. It will also help flush any toxins that are released from the cells, as the negative energy is discharged from the body. If you feel spacey or light-headed, eat some grounding protein—nuts, seeds, or lean meats (preferably organic). I also urge you to eat lots of organic leafy greens, fruits and vegetables. As your body clears out the old, it's going to need healthy building blocks to create healthy proteins to repair and upgrade itself. Give it all the good nutrition you can—and stay away from sugars, grains and processed foods which will depress your immune system and spike your blood sugar. You're doing this to create optimal health and wellness. Support yourself on every level. You'll be much happier you did!

Also remember to be very gentle with yourself as you go through this process. Sometimes, as you clear something, other negative memories begin to emerge—especially if you've experienced significant traumatic events. This is natural and normal. It means that your mind and soul know that you have the tools to handle the emotions. As other images, words or phrases come up, keep a pen and paper handy to write down what you are thinking and feeling so that you can clear those energies next. It is Spirit's way of helping you become completely free!

If you feel completely overwhelmed or stuck and don't feel like you can do this process by yourself, there are resources on my web-site at www.QuantumSoulClearing.com. There you can learn more about personal and group coaching opportunities, home-study audio programs, and monthly Q&A calls, to give you support and guidance as you move forward in your personal journey of transformation and evolution. You don't have to feel alone! There's a whole community of people, just like you, that are committed to themselves, their healing and to each other. Come join us as we heal and grow together.

Chapter 5

Step Three
You Want Me to Download What?
Now For the Really Good Stuff

Now that you've cleared what has been causing you pain, what do you want to create for yourself and your life? What do you need in order to feel whole and alive? How would you like to feel? Wouldn't you like to feel supported, loved, joy, gratitude, empowered? You can. You can have anything your heart desires. Really, you can!

For instance, if you are clearing "fear," as your process, depending on the circumstances that caused your fear, you might choose to download "trust, courage, peacefulness, joy, wholeness, understanding, soul-salve, kindness, friendship, laughter, love from others, love for others, relaxation, right relationships, courtesy, strength, supportiveness and success."

If you are clearing out the frequencies of your ex-lover who cheated on you and left you for another person, you might ask your highest self to download "love, Quantum Source-Light love in all its forms, love from others, love of others, love of self, right relationships, appropriate boundaries, respect of self, respect of others, respect from self, respect from others, kindness, courtesy, courtship, worthiness, wisdom, peace, optimism, confidence, comfort, acceptance, poise, harmony, honest, hope, involvement, joy, gratitude and appreciation, Soul Salve and Cosmic Quantum Salve. These frequencies and others will help re-program the essence of you with better boundaries, and appropriate love frequencies that are a match to another partner who is in alignment with you and your values.

Once the old, negative, energetic charges are removed, you need to download positive frequencies to fill the void created by the removal of the negative. Nature abhors a vacuum! So in order to prevent any of the old stuff from re-creating itself we need to put something special in its place. This is where the Quantum Soul Download and Replacement come in. This is my favorite part of the process because it feels so good!

This final part of the three-step Quantum Soul Clearing process is so freeing and impactful, because it re-programs the cells of the body, the mind, the spirit—every aspect of who you really are.

Make sure you are still connected within to your Divine Core Center and from that place of centeredness and peace ask your highest self and Source to begin downloading the frequencies you want or need in order to feel whole and joyful. Keep asking for what it is you want until you feel like there's nothing more you can ask for and experience.

I've included a list of common positive frequencies that I use with my clients. This list is by no means complete. Whatever you are clearing for yourself may need something that is not listed here. The chart below includes mostly single words. You can use single words or phrases for your download. The point is YOU get to decide what it is you need in order to complete your full healing process. This is how you empower yourself. It is how you feel nurtured, supported and loved. Use as many of these positive frequencies as you want or need, and add anything you'd like at any time. There is no limit to the healing you can experience.

You begin this final process by making sure you are still connected to your Divine Core Center. Once you've connected in to your Highest Self, say, **"Please download** _____," and begin picking and choosing from the words on the positive words list, below, or another other positive frequency you'd like to have included. Ask for everything you want. Choose all the words that you want or need in order to replace the old programming. Add your own phrases that have the deepest meaning for you and convey exactly what you want to experience. Keep adding words until the process feels absolutely complete.

Acclaim	Achievement	Accolades	Affirming
Amazement	Ambition in Balance	Appreciation	Ascendency
Ascension	Assistance	Attunement	Authenticity
Awareness	Beauty	Beneficence	Benevolence
Betterment	Blessings	Bliss	Bounty
Calmness	Caring	Celebration	Certainty
Cheerfulness	Choice	Cleanliness	Comfort
Concern	Confidence	Congratulations	Constructiveness
Consciousness	Consideration	Constancy	Contribution
Cooperation	Cosmic Quantum Salve	Courage	Courtesy
Creativity	Decency	Decisiveness	Delight
Desirable	Desire	Determination	Ease
Ecstasy	Efficiency	Elegance	Encouragement
Endearment	Endeavor	Endorsement	Endurance
Energized	Energy	Enhancement	Enjoyment
Enlightenment	Enlivenment	Enough	Enraptured
Enrichment	Enterprising	Enthusiasm	Equality
Esteem	Ethics	Exaltation	Excellence

Expertise	Exulting	Faith	Fame
Fellowship	Financial Freedom	Forgiveness	Freedom
Friendliness	Fulfillment	Fun	Generosity
Genuineness	Gentleness	Gifts	Giving
Giving Freedom	Glorious	Goodness	Grace
Gratefulness	Gratitude	Guidance	Happiness
Harmony	Health	Heaven	Helpfulness
Honesty	Hope	Hospitality	Impeccability
Improvement	Increase	Incredible	Ingenuity
Innocence	Inspiration	Intelligence	Involvement
Integrity	Intelligence	Joy	Jubilant
Justice	Kind-Heartedness	Kindness	Laughter
Lavishness	Learned	Liberation	Life
Light	Light-Heartedness	Liking	Listening
Love of God	Love of Life	Love of Men	Love of Women
Loyalty	Luck	Lucrative	Luminous
Luxuriant	Luxury	Magnificence	Majesty
Manifesting	Marvelous	Mastery	Mediation
Mercy	Merit	Miracles	Motivation

Money	New	Nirvana	Notable
Noticeable	Nourished	Nurtured	Open-Minded
Openness	Opportunity	Optimism	Order
Originality	Outgoing	Outstanding	Paradise
Pardon	Passion	Patience	Peace
Perseverance	Perspective	Pleasurable	Plenty
Poise	Polite	Possibilities	Potentials
Praise	Preciousness	Productivity	Proficiency
Progress	Promotion	Prosperity	Punctuality
Purification	Purpose	Quantum Source-Light Love in All Its Forms	Quietness
Radiance	Rapture	Readiness	Reassurance
Receiving	Receptivity	Refreshment	Relaxation
Release	Relief	Remarkable	Responsibility
Respect of Self	Respect from Self	Respect for Others	Respect from Others
Restful	Restoration	Results	Reverence
Reward	Rewarding	Rich	Richness
Sacredness	Safe	Satisfaction	Self-Assertive
Self-Awareness	Self-Control	Self-Confidence	Self-Empowerment

Self-Esteem	Self-Love	Self-Respect	Self-Forgiveness
Self-Preservation	Simplicity	Sincerity	Smart
Sobriety	Soul-Salve	Special	Spectacular
Strength	Success	Supportiveness	Sympathy
Succinct	Sufficient	Tact	Thanks
Thorough	Thoughtfulness	Thrive	Timeliness
Tolerance	Tranquility	Transcendence	Triumphant
Trust	Truthfulness	Trustworthiness	Ultimate Freedom
Unconditional Love	Understanding	Unfettered	Unflagging
Upbeat	Upgraded	Uplifted	Upstanding
Usefulness	Validated	Valuable	Valued
Versatile	Vibrant	Virtuous	Vitality
Vivacious	Warmth	Welcome	Well
Wellbeing	Wholeness	Wholesome	Will
Willing	Win	Winner	Wisdom
Wonder	Wonderful	Wonderment	Worth
Worthiness	Worthwhile	Wow	Yea!
Yes	Youthfulness	Zeal	Zest

Once you feel like you've gotten all the frequencies you need, then say:

"Please download any other Quantum Source-Light frequencies that may not have been said but that are needed in any and all languages."

Wait a moment or two for the rest of the positive frequencies to download successfully. Usually people feel an additional "whoosh" of energy as the frequencies enter their bodies. Once that feels complete, then say the next statement as a command:

"Please download, infuse, implement and integrate all these new frequencies and everything they represent. Clear and Remove all old limiting patterns and programs; and replace with all of these New Frequencies and everything they represent at all levels, layers and depths of my Being."

As this portion of the process is occurring, take two or three deep cleansing breaths and notice that with each breath the feeling of those old patterns, energies and programs leaving your body. Imagine any residual energy or energetic pattern or frequency completely disappear and move out of your body, mind and soul. Feel the new, light, positive frequencies simultaneously move in and begin to settle into the cells and tissues energy structures of every aspect of your being. Take a minute or two and enjoy the feelings of the transformation that are happening.

Once that portion of the transformative process feels complete, then say out-loud with authority, again as a command:

"Activate, Synchronize, Harmonize, and Optimize all of these new frequencies and everything they represent. Please integrate

and anchor them in at all levels, layers and depths of my Being.
Then, please apply them all as functional skill sets."

You will feel all of these new, positive frequencies solidify into place. At this point I usually ask my clients to quickly reflect back to what we were clearing to see if there is any energetic charge at all. If there is any "charge" at all, I ask them to rate that "charge" of a scale of 0 to 10; 10 being active and causing negative physical reactions, and zero being completely gone and feeling light and joyful.

If there is any "charge," I ask them to determine if it is a secondary feeling or frequency that need to be addressed, or if it is the same one. Almost every time, if there is any charge at all, it is a secondary issue that is now able to be addressed. Interestingly, this secondary charge is often much bigger, once we get into it, than the first thing that got cleared. It's like peeling back an onion, each layer reveals another, and sometimes those inner layers are even stronger, and more smelly, than the outer layers!

When you check in and it still feels like the energy of the first thing you were clearing is still active, it may be that one of three things is happening:

1. That the issue was so big that it just needed to be done a second time to do a completely mop-up. Some things are like that.
2. It may be that you weren't completely connected to your highest self and connected to the power that is the source of the healing. If you are new to this process, it is very easy to lose connection with your Divine Core Center and be in your head as you read the statements. It takes some practice to anchor yourself into your solar plexus, stay connected with Source energy, and read at the same time! Don't give up, you can do it.
3. It could be that you are clearing something that isn't really the thing that needs to be cleared. For example, you may have had

a conflict with another person and you think that clearing that conflict or that person is what needs to be done. However, the primary thing that needs to be cleared might be "feeling judged unfairly." This is why it is so important to dig deep within to identify what the *real* underlying feelings really are. That's where the healing and freedom lie.

Remember, if you need help, you can always contact us at www. QuantumSoulClearing.com to get some coaching to help you through the process and support you with your healing process.

For the majority of people, as they check in, there is absolutely nothing left of what was being cleared at all. Instead, there is a feeling of peace, happiness, joyfulness, centeredness and feeling energized, and a feeling of being completely and fully alive, as never before!

Many people report that when this process is complete, the energy they've been dealing with feels like it happened to another person. Or that looking at that event is now like looking at it as if it's a movie of someone else's experience, instead of being in the picture themselves. Often, they can't even remember what it is that was cleared after a few days. That's how you know that something has been fully cleared—you have trouble remembering what it was that was cleared. That's pretty resolved! And that really is the intent of this whole process: to clear it as if it had never happened at all.

When I'm working with a client I also get to feel their feelings of joy and relief. I have to admit I get a real "high" out of how joyful they feel, as well. It is so gratifying to know that a big road block that someone has been struggling with, sometimes for years, is now resolved and that they can easily move on with their lives. Better yet, because the thing that has been holding them back is now gone, they can begin to go after and create their biggest dreams and desires!

I love that the person has a tool that they can use for the rest of their lives to immediately get rid of negative charges when they comes up.

Now you do too! Now is the time to refer back to the list of negative feelings in chapter one that you would like to clear, and go through this process for yourself. There's no time like the present to begin changing your life for the better. What's stopping you?

CHAPTER 6

I'M NOT REALLY SURE WHAT I'M FEELING, I JUST DON'T FEEL GOOD!

You've learned how to clear specific feelings and situations. But what if you can't put a specific word on exactly what you're feeling? Sometimes we are so caught up in a situation or the chaos of life, we don't stop to identify the different parts of what we are feeling. Or perhaps you know something is wrong, but you just cannot identify the specific word. I believe that is one of the big draw-backs of the English language. It doesn't adequately identify our exact feelings. How do you clear something that is there, but can't be exactly identified?

Often, a feeling cannot be described in just one word. You may have to use a sentence or a string of associated words together to more closely identify what the energetic charge is for you. Use whatever words most closely associate the feelings that you're having and begin clearing them.

Often, it may feel like you're clearing and clearing and just circling around the real root of the problem. Or you just cannot put a specific word, phrase or label on the specific energetic that you can feel.

That's OK. When that happens, take a deep cleansing breath. Close your eyes and drop down into your Divine Core Center. Connect in with your highest self and with God/Source and begin the clearing statements, while holding attention on that feeling.

In this scenario, I will say, "Clear *this feeling* and everything it represents," then go through the whole Quantum Soul Clearing Process, using the words, "this feeling," while trying to stay focused on the energy you're clearing.

It can get a little tricky, though, to hold the energy of that particular feeling as you go through the process, because as you go through this process the energy is resolved. It just melts away! Just trust that your Highest Self and God/Source are helping you resolve this issue and that you will be free of it. You know the process is successful when you no longer feel that energetic charge.

Often, it is very beneficial to hire a Quantum Soul Clearing Coach to help you get to the core of the problem, if you are having difficulties getting to the bottom of a problem. It is almost impossible to see our own blind spots. Our coaches are trained to help you cut to the core of the problem and resolve the root. A good coach can help you cut through the clutter and gently help you focus on what the real issues are. This helps save you time and frustration, and helps you create the life you really want more quickly, which is really what you want, right?

For a list of qualified coaches, please contact us at http://quantumsoulclearing.com/contact, and we will put you in contact with one of our amazing coaches!

Chapter 7

Can I Do This For Other People?

Now that you've gone through the whole process for yourself, how are you feeling? Most people report a feeling of immense relief. They say they feel like they have dropped a huge weight. They are flying, floating, and feeling connected to Source in a way they've never felt before. They feel excited and refreshed—full of hope for what comes next. And they're mostly excited because they realize they can begin working on all the baggage they are consciously aware of. What a profound feeling of empowerment! You have a tool in your hands that can free you from your past! Isn't this wonderful?

The next thing I'm usually asked is, "Can I use this with my husband, children, parents, co-workers, boss, and everyone I know?"

The answer is yes—and no. You can learn to do this process with others, but it must be done with knowledge and care. In fact, I have developed a training program to teach and certify other practitioners to use the Quantum Soul Clearing Process. For more information about this certification process, please contact me at Michelle@ QuantumSoulClearing.com.

Working on behalf of another can be very fulfilling. However, there are some specific, ethical ground rules that *must* be adhered to. We have to acknowledge and respect other people's boundaries and processes. We may think we know what is best for another person, but that person has to *want* to make the changes themselves, or we are interfering with another person's life path, and being co-dependent. That's out of integrity. And it can have significant karmic repercussions for you. You have to have impeccable honesty and integrity when working on behalf of another person.

Webster's dictionary defines "proxy" as: *Power or authority that is given to allow a person to act for someone else—usually used in the phrase 'by proxy.'* This is a very large responsibility and one that should be taken very thoughtfully and seriously.

You must be truly clear yourself before you begin.

It is critically important to know if you are using this technology to try to control someone else's behaviors and experiences to make yourself feel better. That is completely out of integrity with who you really are. And it won't work. You *cannot* make someone do something that they don't deeply and authentically want to do.

Everyone on this planet has the free will to choose for themselves how they feel and act no matter what. It is *your* responsibility to know how you feel and how you may be being triggered and reactive to another person's actions toward you. By clearing the negative feelings that are triggered in **you first**—before you try to change another— you change the interactional experience. Once the old energy that created those interactions is gone, the other person cannot interact with you in the same way, because there's nothing there to attach to. Often, after you've cleared yourself, the other person changes as well. It has been the energetic charge that the negative interactions have created, that colors how you see and behave with that person.

My suggestion is to go within, and identify what feelings are being triggered in you first. Clear the feelings and the triggers that are affecting *you.* Clear everything you can that bothers you about the other person: their behaviors, your judgments, your beliefs of their "wrongness," until there is absolutely no triggering energy in you for what is happening. Identify the feelings that are created within you by the judgments from and of the other person. Go deep! It is your responsibility to work on yourself first and foremost. Once *your* energy is clear, then you can check-in with your Highest Self to ask if it is highest and best.

My advice (if you were to ask for it) is to give that other person a copy of this book and let them do their own work, while you do what you need to do for yourself. That way, you honor the other person as a master of their experiences and life, you take responsibility for your own experiences and life, and you don't inadvertently incur negative karmic repercussions.

If you are going to do this work for someone else, is always important to get the other person's verbal permission to do this work for them. However, there will be times when there are small children or the sick and infirm who cannot do this work for themselves. In circumstances where it is not possible to get the person's verbal permission do the following steps:

1. Get yourself centered.
2. Focus your attention within yourself and connect with your Divine Core Center.
3. Say your connecting prayer (just like in Chapter Two when we first started). Ask to be connected to the person's Highest Self.
4. Wait until you feel the connection and then ask the person's Highest Self if it is highest and best (I often use the word "optimal") if you can work with the person.

If the Highest Self says no—or there is resistance, you have to trust that it is for a reason and honor that "no."

There are many people whose highest selves have said no to me when I've asked to work with them at the request of another family member or friend. That means that they are not ready for the work to be done yet. And that's okay. That's when I work with the person asking for the work to be done in order to clear the charges around whatever is occurring. It's not that the other family member or friend doesn't need the work. Usually it means that the person asking for someone else to be cleared has work of their own to do first!

If I do get the permission to proceed, I thank the person's Highest Self. I begin my connecting within statement or prayer. Again, mine is, *"Mother/Father, God/Goddess, Creator; Absolute, Ultimate, Infinite, Radiant-Golden, Quantum Source Light and I are ONE, we work together as a unified co-creative team. By the Power, the Authority and Divinity inherent within me, through my connection with and Oneness as Absolute, Ultimate, Infinite, Radiant, Golden Quantum Source Light, please prep to work and clear."* (Feel free to use your own!)

Then I say the following: *"Please prepare, place, establish and strengthen a Quantum Source-Light containment and protection field around me, a separate containment and protection field around _____, and additional containment and protection fields around all our loved ones, individually. Clear and remove all types of extra souls, dark portals, toxic streams and decaying universes, all their effects and everything they represent from in, on, around and through all of these containment and protection fields. Clear all negative motivations, blocks and interferences and blocks to positive expressions that any of us may be running. Clear all sparks, programs, issues and challenges that we are running in all times, places and spaces."*

Wait for a few moments to feel those fields being built and placed around everyone and that the negative energy is cleared and removed. Then proceed to the clearing statements.

When doing the work for another, there are two ways to phrase the statements. The first is to say, *"As proxy for* _____," and say the statements the same way you would use the statements for yourself—in the first person. That way you are literally "standing in" as the person you're working with. I often feel the physical sensations for the person I'm working with when I do this. It's as if my body is actually doing the processing for the other person. I mention this so that if it happens that way for you, you won't be completely surprised! It can be a little disconcerting if you're not used to doing proxy work for another person.

The second way is to say the clearing statements on behalf of the person. For example, "On behalf of (Fill in with the person's name), clear _____ (and everything is represents throughout Michelle's body, energy bodies and Michelle, all her systems . . ." and so on. I've done the statements both ways and they are both equally effective. I will often feel the shifts for people this way, too, but they are not usually as strong, and there is a bit more "space" between me and the person I'm doing the work for.

Once you've gone through the whole process, along with the forgiveness statements and the down-loading of what you want the person to receive, it is very important to disconnect your energy from the other person's energy. There are several ways to do this. Two of my favorite ways are listed below. You may also have your own methods of cutting energetic ties that you may be familiar with. Feel free to use those, too.

The first is simply to thank Spirit for the experience and the help you received in getting the work done for the other person. Then ask that your energy fields be completely separated and that appropriate boundaries be re-established immediately. You can actually feel the energies separate and that you become two separate people again!

A second way is to call upon Archangel Michael and ask that he use his Sword of Light and Truth to sever any and all cords that are still connecting you to the other person. Thank Source for the assistance you've received in the clearing process, then, as you envision Archangel Michael using his sword to sever those ties, use your own hands in a cutting motion to clear the auric field around you. Don't forget to go around and over your head, down your legs and across the bottom of each foot. Then ask for appropriate boundaries to be placed between you and the other person.

I teach weekend intensives for those who are interested in becoming Quantum Soul Clearing Coaches. Please contact me through my web-site at http://www.quantumsoulclearing.com for more information about my training and certification programs.

Conclusion

As I end this book, I want to thank you for spending your valuable time with me learning about the Quantum Soul Clearing Process. As you can see, you can use this Spiritual technology to more easily make positive changes in your life and empower yourself to create the most compelling life possible that you can imagine. By using this process, you can release the emotional pain and suffering that have imprisoned you and free yourself from the past. Ultimately, you can forgive yourself and others, and feel more joy, peace of mind and ultimate freedom.

I know from personal experience how ignoring and stuffing emotional pain can affect your health and well-being—even to the point of losing your life. There is an enormous price to pay at many levels by not working through our old emotional baggage to erase the pain and suffering we experience.

Often, we think that we have dealt with our "stuff," and then are surprised when we are blind-sided by it again. Or we wonder why we really don't feel as happy as we think we could, but don't know how to get to the root of our dissatisfaction. With this process you now have tools to finally leave the past behind and feel that happiness and vibrant well-being from within.

I believe we were meant to live joyously, and freely, connected within to Spirit, and outwardly with each other. That's not to say that life doesn't challenge us at times, because we would never have opportunities to grow and know true happiness. However, I believe that by changing our chaotic and conflicted internal programs, beliefs and feelings, we can manifest anything we desire: self-worth, wonderful, supportive relationships; financial abundance; inner peace of mind; connection with Source; a career that seems like play instead of work; and fulfillment at all levels.

I believe that whatever you choose to create in your life is only limited by the extent of your imagination. If you can dream it you can have it. All it takes is your inner thoughts, feelings and beliefs to be in crystal clear alignment with your actions on a consistent basis. Within the pages of this book are powerful tools to create that alignment and success.

I want to extend a 30-day challenge to you. Every day for the next 30 days, choose just one negative feeling or event that still has an energetic hook. (You can clear more than one if you'd like.) Choose something from the list of what you don't want that you created in the first chapter of this book.

Identify the feeling or feelings that you wrote about in the first exercise in Chapter One from you "don't want" statements. Do a complete clearing statement to release the energy from it. Then journal about what you experienced as you did the clearing.

It will only take you about 15-20 minutes a day to do this process. At the end of 30 days, see just how far you've come. Notice how your relationships with yourself and others are vastly improved. Best of all, feel how much more personal peace, joy, and self-love you will experience. Begin to create *your* magnificent life!

Author's Message

I want to thank you for having the courage and determination to take the steps necessary to create a life of clarity, personal peace and joy. Each small step forward affects you, your family, your friends and, ultimately, the entire world. I believe that we can have world peace—but it can only be done one step at a time and it starts within each of us, individually.

The truth is that we have a powerful energetic impact on each other. As we become clearer, more centered and grounded, and begin to divest ourselves of the old emotional baggage that no longer serves us, we more positively affect each other. As we grow and evolve, reaching for our ultimate, infinite potential, we actually model and give silent (or not so silent) permission to others to do the same.

I believe that we all have a unique purpose that we've come here to fulfill. Mine is to share this message of hope, transformation and love with you, and help you find the courage and empowerment to life your life fully and ultimately free. My hope and intention is that you find what brings you the most joy in your life and then live *your* soul's purpose.

If you've enjoyed or benefitted from the information in this book, please pass it on to your friends of family members. Give a copy as a gift to those you love and care for. Share this message and the Spiritual technology it contains so that others can benefit from it, as well. That is how we can create more joy and love in the world. Visit my web-site and sign up for the Universal Explosion of Joy and Transformation movement. Join our rapidly growing Quantum Soul Clearing community and connect in our free membership site with other like-minded people from around the world. Go to www. QuantumSoulClearing.com/Membership. As a member, you'll receive valuable updates, advance notice of events and discounts for products, and services. You'll also find many helpful resources to help you grow and evolve as we move from the old paradigm world into the new.

It is my hope that I have positively affected your life and given you the tools to change your life for the better. It is up to you to take those tools and apply them in your life every day.

I would love to hear how this information has helped you or changed your life. Please drop me a note at Michelle@QuantumSoulClearing. com and tell me how this book has impacted you. And for more incredible products and services, to help support you on your journey of self-discovery and evolution, go to http://www. QuantumSoulClearing.com. I look forward to hearing from you soon.

My Blessings of Love and Light to You!

Michelle

Client Testimonials

I've received hundreds of client testimonials over the years, and continue to receive testimonials every day from people who are profoundly changed using this Spiritual technology. All have touched my heart, and many have made me cry with tears of happiness, humility and gratitude for the ability to help others empower and change their lives. Nothing brings me more joy than to watch people heal from their past, then take wings and fly, making their goals and dreams a reality.

I would like to share just a few of those testimonials with you, so you can hear what this work has done for others. Here they are in their own words:

"I would like to speak about Michelle Manning-Kogler's work both from the point of view of my personal growth and from the point of view of someone who held senior-level administrative positions in fairly large organizations for almost thirty years.

Briefly, after some years as a university professor, I became the head of a large public library system, and then eventually a dean at a California community college, where in addition to my own areas of responsibility,

I was part of the senior administrative team leading the college as a whole.

Over the years I came to realize that "dead spots" in the organization—negative or bureaucratic behavior that was frustrating to customers, interpersonal conflicts, resistance to effective decision-making and organizational change, lack of productivity—typically involved people (employees or managers) who were personally dysfunctional: lacking in self-awareness, and (often unconsciously) acting out their inner issues at work. I also found that the usual training in better customer service, more effective work habits and interpersonal behavior modification didn't do much to change things.

Unfortunately, I had retired by the time I began working with Michelle Manning-Kogler. But I have often thought how much Michelle's transformation and Quantum Soul Clearing Processes would have helped me throughout my career, as well as my colleagues and employees—and how much that would have improved the productivity, effectiveness, and adaptability of the whole organization.

I began working with Michelle in 2005. Almost on a whim, I scheduled a telephone appointment with her. I was dealing with a number of life changes, but I had always handled my own problems and was not sure that spiritually-based work would help me. I was astonished by how "right on the money," powerful, and transformative that first session was.

Since then, I have worked with Michelle to clear various emotional, interpersonal, or physical patterns and blockages, and in every case her work was extremely helpful and effective. I am far more balanced, energetic, compassionate, and creative in my thinking than I have ever been. I have built a successful new career as a writer and yoga teacher, and a new and happy marriage.

One of the things I appreciate about Michelle is her good-humored, pragmatic and down-to-earth approach to what might seem esoteric and strange. I believe in the holistic view that mind, body, energy, and spirit are all interconnected. Michelle's work goes right to the spiritual core of that whole being, and I think that is why it is so effective. In my experience, superficial or external approaches don't really get at the root of a problem and therefore don't make permanent changes.

I can personally testify that her approach, and the various modalities she employs, are effective. And I can also say as a retired administrator that I can think of numerous instances in which her work would have transformed not only individuals but the organization as a whole."

R. Thompson, Ph.D.

New York

* * *

"I had the good fortune recently to personally experience Michelle's Quantum Clearing. This I now know; if you want a new perspective you need to embrace a new way to take action. Give yourself the gift of participation in Michelle's Quantum Clearing expertise and gain a whole new understanding of the areas that block the realization of the true you. Not sure, skeptical? I was too, but the act of commitment to a session is all you risk. The rewards last a lifetime. I had not one but two MAJOR insights in less than an hour. There are 168 hours in a week—schedule one with Michelle—you'll be glad you did, and your life will thank you".

Dan Robinson, CPLC

* * *

"Michelle has a special gift. She is able to tap into that Universal Field and be in touch with the subtle vibrations in that field. She has a keen sense of what needs to be cleared from our auras or what negative vibrations are emanating outward from each of us.

She posses a technique, *The Quantum Soul Clearing Process*, that really does clear out those unwanted blocks, and replace them with the desired energies that endable us to move forward.

I was gifted with the opportunity to experience a clearing from Michelle in a very small and intimate group setting. During the process, I immediately felt lighter and had increased energy and vitality, and a feeling of joyous well-being as we worked to clear and release the unwanted issues I was dealing with. I also experienced an incoming flood of beautiful and creative images, many of which I have been using in my artwork to heal others!

Immediately after the session, I continued to feel lighter and released from negative energies and influences. I have noticed over the days following that I have gained much greater clarity regarding the direction I want to pursue in my life's work. I feel a deeper sense of my purpose and renewd energy to forge ahead!"

Marcy Lifavi, Artist

California

*   *   *

"My work with Michelle Manning-Kogler and the Quantum Soul Clearing Process has been profoud, fascinating, and a life changing experience. It has created more healing and progress in one month than a decade of other therapeutic techniques that I have used in the past. As a Physician/Scientist, I was skeptical at first, but my intuition *strongly urged me to continue. So I suspended all the "logic" I had been trained with for many years and stepped off the cliff into the abyss of the unknown.*

I am incredibly thankful that I did so, because I starting to find the life that I have dreamed of for so many, many years. I feel truly blessed to have encountered and to be working with this incredibly gifted healer."

C. Catzavelos, PhD

Quebec, Canada

*   *   *

"When Michelle first asked me to write down a few of my experiences with her and the work she does, and how they have impacted my life—my first thoughts were: "Michelle literally—in every sense of the word—SAVED my life—not only my physical body, but also my spirit and my soul." To merely say she has "made a difference" in my life would be an understatement. Along with all the healing, of my body, learning about myself in every possible aspect of my life—physical, mental, spiritual, past experiences, who I really am, what I really am, who I have the potential to be—the list goes on and on and on—also came the teaching that I needed to continue to ". . . heal thyself" (Luke 4:23). It is very difficult for me to even put into words the things that I feel in my heart.

Michelle is an incredibly gifted woman, with many, many different gifts and abilities. However—she has never just taken them for granted, and has spent her entire lifetime studying, learning, researching, seeking the truth, and always striving to progress, and learn more. She is a gift to the world, and a person with unique talents that she strives to share with everyone she can, on a daily basis. Michelle has changed the lives of countless people throughout the years, and I am thankful that I have been one of the very lucky people who have been given the opportunity to work with Michelle.

I have had the privilege of working with Michelle in many different ways, for years, in many different settings and situations. Some of these include: energy work and healing, both physical and mental, clearing work, SRT (Spiritual Response Technique), use of essential oils, homeopathic medicine, and most recently, lots of testing with wonderful equipment and great expertise in finding out exactly what is going on with my body, and exactly what my body needs. Today—I gave these results to my personal Physician, and he totally agreed with her findings 100%!!! He is doing blood work, to satisfy the "medical community requirements"—and has already identified many of these problems in past years, but has never been able to "put them all together"—because of the missing puzzle pieces. Michelle was able to find the missing links that brings it all together, and identifies many, many questions regarding multiple, life-long health issues. To say that I am thrilled beyond what words can express is the understatement of the century. Some people would feel overwhelmed and discouraged with all the things Michelle has discovered about me these past few years but I find this so exciting as there is FINALLY light at the end of the tunnel!

I do not discount any of the work I have done with Michelle these past few years—but this feels like we know the whole truth. I feel like I can say I am "experienced" in multiple health issues, throughout my life, including 22 surgeries, 30+ aspiration pneumonia's since November 2007, and a life long history of hundreds of cases of bronchitis, pneumonia (bacterial and viral), along with many other health issues. Some of those include Pulmonary Emboli three different times, multiple auto immune disorders, mood swings, depression, and feeling like I'd never feel healthy again. However—these past few years, my working with Michelle has kept me on a steady, mostly uphill climb—and now I feel like I've just been given a new lease of life!!!

In the past, Michelle has done a lot of "Clearing Work" with me with the Quantum Soul Clearing Process. We not only worked with problems and limitations that were known to me, but also discovered traumatic things that had happened to me in the past that my mind had totally blocked out. She was wonderful—a "safe person," non-judgmental, caring, healing, loving, gentle, patient, understanding, giving, and gave me the gift of leaving these things in the past. Not only did that help me mentally and spiritually, but also made a huge difference in helping my body start on the road to recovery, also. I have learned from her that all of it is inter-connected—that you must be healthy to heal mentally and spiritually, and you must be healthy mentally and spiritually to heal physically. Some of these experiences have been immediate, and others a long, careful process, all while continuing to learn and progress.

What I did not realized was that an added benefit of all of this was preparing me to be a better, stronger, healthier person, with "tools" to help me withstand the most horrific test of my entire life. Although we did not know that one day, I would face this—I know with all of my heart and soul that I was only able to survive this chain of events because of Michelle, her healing powers, and her teaching, her example and her love.

In 2006 and 2008, I lost first my father, and then my mother. I had been their caregiver for almost five years, and my own health suffered greatly during that time. But Michelle was with me every step of the way, and in the past two years has played a most important role in helping me recover my health and well being. But the worst was yet to come.

In September 2010, my 30 year old son took his own life. Michelle was again with me every step of the way, physically, emotionally, mentally and spiritually. Her love, caring, compassion, and the many things she has taught me and done for me came back when I needed them the most. I have NEVER experienced greater pain and anguish in my entire life! There are no words to express the depth of pain and raw emotion I have felt since losing my precious son. Of course, I have relied greatly on her guidance, but I know for sure I could not have survived this great trauma health wise—physically and emotionally, without her great efforts in my behalf. I can never truly express my love and gratitude to her for these wonderful gifts. I thank God for her every day of my life. She has helped me find "my highest power" (which can and will continue to grow) and my life will go on and progress.

One of the greatest things that I know to be true as I try and express my feelings about Michelle and the many great gifts she has given me is this: I AM ONLY ONE OF MANY PEOPLE MICHELLE HAS HELPED!

So, in conclusion, I pose several questions:

Has Michelle had a huge impact upon my life??? Yes!!!

Has Michelle changed my life significantly??? Yes!!!

Am I the person I am today due in great part to Michelle??? Yes!!!

Am I alive today because of Michelle??? Yes!!!

Would I recommend Michelle and her services to anyone??? YES!

(Even the stubborn ones that took a while to teach—and believe in her work, like me.)

Is my life better today because of Michelle, her work and her example??? Yes!!!

I know that Michelle will continue to grow, to learn new things, and reach greater heights and I plan on being around for a long time to learn more and more of the things she has to teach me. The learning never ends. To say a simple "Thank You" does not seem like enough, so I will end with the phrase Michelle has lovingly taught me to say: "I gratefully accept this gift you have given me. Thank you."

M. E. Ford,

West Valley City, UT

*   *   *

Dear Michelle,

Just a few moments ago I finished listening to the replay of your recent call, and I am moved and inspired to reach out to you, to share my experience.

I consider myself a lightworker with innate and valuable gifts, however undeveloped and underused. I consider myself a member of the lightworker's community, and as such I try to listen and participate in as many calls and meditations as I can.

However, I am a super busy stay at home mother of four, and as you can imagine the actual time I have to spend in these types of calls is pretty limited. I find that I can be pretty hard on myself for not making more time to participate in calls like these, most particularly the programs that [the host] puts together.

For some reason, this morning I decided that everything could wait— the laundry, dishes, yoga, the dog walk, housework, paying the bills, working on this online course I am taking, everything. I usually have a long internal struggle with what needs to happen next; I find half my mornings are spent walking around the house I circles trying to decide what task has precedence. But this morning—very strangely!—all that fell away and I settled myself out on my porch to listen to the replay of this call. I had never heard of you before, I did no research on the subject of the call . . . it was as if it was "laid on me" to take these two hours to listen.

Michelle, I was struck on such a profound level, to so many things that were said. My visualization and experience of the connecting meditation literally blew me away. I was engulfed in the most pristine, pale yellow gold with sparkling pale pink swirls and embellishments. I felt the weight of the hands of so many loved ones across the globe, as if they were actually holding my hands. Their faces were so clear in my mind's eye as this golden pink light enveloped them as well, and swooped on to other faces that I didn't recognize. I assume they were the faces of others on the call.

I connected so profoundly to the calls with [the two people you worked with]. Although I knew you were focusing on their energy systems, it was like every word you said was unique to me, created specifically to me. I heard your words in my head before you said them, in some instances. The image of the sand spilling from the hourglass—it was like you read my mind!!

When we were waiting on the line for Denise, I was asking myself what I would have put before you, had I been the one on the call. Her statement of feeling anxious, waiting for something to happen but not knowing what, knowing SOMETHING is happening but not knowing how she played a part . . . . it was almost verbatim to what was going through my head. Then as the work with her began, I became extremely cold, shivering and uncomfortable. I had to get up and I found myself pacing around and unable to focus on what I needed. I ended up getting my bathrobe and putting it over me and resettling on the porch, after sitting in this seat and that seat, trying to get comfortable again! I can't explain what I experienced on the call. I did at one point have what can be described as small, local explosions of energy that send tendrils of the clearest light tingling over the left side of my body.

I don't know why I feel like I need to explain to you every detail I can conjure. Maybe I need to get it down and send it out into the world to make it more than a dream. I keep thinking of what Dumbledore said to Harry [in Harry Potter]: "Of course this is happening in your head, but why should that make it less real?"

I don't know what happened this morning—who or what guided me to that call. I can't explain what level of connection I experienced today. All I know is, the only way I can explain it is, something was at work today. My guides, angels, my intentions led me to you and to the clearing work we did today. I want to thank you from the bottom of my heart for your commitment to raising the level of light and love on our earth. Thank you for the generosity of your time and gifts. I feel so very proud of you. I know that must sound so silly, to be proud of someone who doesn't even know I exist—but I am! I'm proud that you have developed your gifts so beautifully.

You are doing profound and sacred work. I am honored to be, even on the most remote level, a thread in the web that connects me to you, and all the light workers.

Thank you again. I will honor your gifts I received today by carrying the truth of them in my heart.

With all that I am,

Summer M. Williams

Today I really was totally and unabashedly literally wiped off my feet. I always have some shift after every call. TODAY!!! Having listened to Michelle Manning—Kogler I moved lifelong baggage that has been hanging around for centuries I'm sure. I have spent over 20 years working on developing my spirituality and doing personal and professional healing, I have never moved anything so powerful. I was crying, laughing, shaking, sobbing, you name it—I did it. I know I have been carrying many lifetimes and especially this one with stomach and digestion issues, difficulty digesting, life off course, so it all makes sense today why I hold all my love and relationships at a distance, the fear of rejection can be so deeply buried and impact in so many different ways. It all came flooding up and out today thanks to you and your commitment to help heal us all.

I am feeling so overwhelmed with emotion I can't think straight and am probably making very little sense.

Please know that my love and the love of all generations before and after me is flooding your way, even my dear old doggie got in on the action, he wandered in and lay done in front of me just watching over me, he knows something big has happened.

Love & Light to you—May God Bless and keep you in his loving arms always.

Janet

Acknowledgements

Many people have contributed to this book, both directly and indirectly. Without them this book would never have been possible.

I first want to thank Stephanie Sorcha Bray, a dear friend and colleague. Her brilliance and faith in Source was the very beginning of the clearing statements. Sorcha is the person who called one day several years ago and asked, "Can you check in on something for me? I've just cleared something and want to make sure it's *really* 100% cleared." And with that the Quantum Soul Clearing Process was born.

I want to thank Susan Hayward, another dear friend and colleague. Her insights and input from her years of Spiritual training, professional coaching, and expansive connection to the unseen worlds further enhanced and birthed this work.

I want to thank my husband, Dennis, for his support in my being able to follow my dreams. Without his love, financial support, and encouragement to do what I love, this book would never have been possible. I love you and appreciate the sacrifices you've made over the years to support me in achieving my dreams.

I want to thank my two daughters, Brittany and Shallice for listening to my joys and triumphs, my fears and perceived failures, and always encouraging me and believing in myself and my dreams. They've always been my most ardent supporters. I love you more than words can express.

I want to thank my parents and family for their love and influence in my life. Without them I wouldn't even be here sharing this message with the world, nor would I have the unique genetics that allow my gifts to flourish. I love you and appreciate you.

I want to thank all the authors and teachers I have had throughout my lifetime who have shared their knowledge and wisdom with me and helped shape my beliefs. They have indirectly contributed to this book through their impact on my life. I thank you for your brilliance and your courage to live your lives as a model for me to become who I am today.

I want to thank Balboa Press and my editors for helping me create this gorgeous book. Their guidance through the process of publishing has been invaluable. I appreciate you so much!

I want to thank all my mastermind team members for their expert coaching, and un-ending, patient input and insights in how to bring this message into the world. I am eternally grateful for you. Their insights and input into how I can make this work better have been a such a gift.

I want to thank God Source and my Non-physical teams whom I rely on daily for their work with me and my clients. Their powerful presence has gifted my life in so many ways. The magic of our work together blesses and heals me every day of my life. I am in such gratitude and appreciation that they have chosen to work with me and through me to help others.

And I want to thank you, dear reader, for your willingness to buy this book and take the information into your life. May you be uplifted and blessed as you take this information into your life to change and transform your life.

APPENDIX
LIST OF POSITIVE WORDS

Abundance	Ability	Acceleration	Acceptance
Acclaim	Achievement	Accolades	Affirming
Amazement	Ambition in Balance	Appreciation	Ascendency
Ascension	Assistance	Attunement	Authenticity
Awareness	Beauty	Beneficence	Benevolence
Betterment	Blessings	Bliss	Bounty
Calmness	Caring	Celebration	Certainty
Cheerfulness	Choice	Cleanliness	Comfort
Concern	Confidence	Congratulations	Constructiveness
Consciousness	Consideration	Constancy	Contribution
Cooperation	Cosmic Quantum Salve	Courage	Courtesy
Creativity	Decency	Decisiveness	Delight
Desirable	Desire	Determination	Ease
Ecstasy	Efficiency	Elegance	Encouragement
Endearment	Endeavor	Endorsement	Endurance

Energized	Energy	Enhancement	Enjoyment
Enlightenment	Enlivenment	Enough	Enraptured
Enrichment	Enterprising	Enthusiasm	Equality
Esteem	Ethics	Exaltation	Excellence
Expertise	Exulting	Faith	Fame
Fellowship	Financial Freedom	Forgiveness	Freedom
Friendliness	Fulfillment	Fun	Generosity
Genuineness	Gentleness	Gifts	Giving
Giving Freedom	Glorious	Goodness	Grace
Gratefulness	Gratitude	Guidance	Happiness
Harmony	Health	Heaven	Helpfulness
Honesty	Hope	Hospitality	Impeccability
Improvement	Increase	Incredible	Ingenuity
Innocence	Inspiration	Intelligence	Involvement
Integrity	Intelligence	Joy	Jubilant
Justice	Kind-Heartedness	Kindness	Laughter
Lavishness	Learned	Liberation	Life
Light	Light-Heartedness	Liking	Listening

Love of God	Love of Life	Love of Men	Love of Women
Loyalty	Luck	Lucrative	Luminous
Luxuriant	Luxury	Magnificence	Majesty
Manifesting	Marvelous	Mastery	Mediation
Mercy	Merit	Miracles	Motivation
Money	New	Nirvana	Notable
Noticeable	Nourished	Nurtured	Open-Minded
Openness	Opportunity	Optimism	Order
Originality	Outgoing	Outstanding	Paradise
Pardon	Passion	Patience	Peace
Perseverance	Perspective	Pleasurable	Plenty
Poise	Polite	Possibilities	Potentials
Praise	Preciousness	Productivity	Proficiency
Progress	Promotion	Prosperity	Punctuality
Purification	Purpose	Quantum Source-Light Love in All Its Forms	Quietness
Radiance	Rapture	Readiness	Reassurance
Receiving	Receptivity	Refreshment	Relaxation
Release	Relief	Remarkable	Responsibility

Respect of Self	Respect from Self	Respect for Others	Respect from Others
Restful	Restoration	Results	Reverence
Reward	Rewarding	Rich	Richness
Sacredness	Safe	Satisfaction	Self-Assertive
Self-Awareness	Self-Control	Self-Confidence	Self-Empowerment
Self-Esteem	Self-Love	Self-Respect	Self-Forgiveness
Self-Preservation	Simplicity	Sincerity	Smart
Sobriety	Soul-Salve	Special	Spectacular
Strength	Success	Supportiveness	Sympathy
Succinct	Sufficient	Tact	Thanks
Thorough	Thoughtfulness	Thrive	Timeliness
Tolerance	Tranquility	Transcendence	Triumphant
Trust	Truthfulness	Trustworthiness	Ultimate Freedom
Unconditional Love	Understanding	Unfettered	Unflagging
Upbeat	Upgraded	Uplifted	Upstanding
Usefulness	Validated	Valuable	Valued
Versatile	Vibrant	Virtuous	Vitality
Vivacious	Warmth	Welcome	Well

Wellbeing	Wholeness	Wholesome	Will
Willing	Win	Winner	Wisdom
Wonder	Wonderful	Wonderment	Worth
Worthiness	Worthwhile	Wow	Yea!
Yes	Youthfulness	Zeal	Zest

LIST OF NEGATIVE WORDS AND FEELINGS

abandoned	abhor	abused	accursed
accused	addicted	afraid	aggravated
aggressive	alarmed	alone	angry
anguish	annoyed	antagonistic	anxious
apathetic	apprehensive	argumentative	artificial
ashamed	assaulted	at a loss	at risk
atrocious	attacked	aversion	avoided
awful	awkward	bad	badgered
baffled	banned	barren	bashful
beaten	belittled	berated	betrayed
bewildered	bitched at	bitter	bizarre
blacklisted	blackmailed	blamed	bleak
blown away	blur	bored	boring
bossed-around	bothered	bothersome	bounded
boxed-in	broken	bruised	brushed-off
bugged	bullied	bummed	bummed out
burdened	burdensome	burned	burned-out

caged in	careless	chaotic	chased
cheated	cheated on	chicken	claustrophobic
clingy	closed	clueless	clumsy
coaxed	codependent	coerced	cold
cold-hearted	combative	commanded	compared
competitive	compulsive	conceited	concerned
condescended to	confined	conflicted	confronted
conned	consumed	contemplative	contempt
contemptuous	contentious	controlled	convicted
cornered	corralled	cowardly	crabby
cramped	cranky	crap	crappy
crazy	creeped out	creepy	critical
criticized	cross	crowded	cruddy
crummy	crushed	cut-down	cynical
damaged	damned	dangerous	dark
dazed	dead	deceived	deep
defamed	defeated	defective	defenseless
defensive	defiant	deficient	deflated
degraded	dehumanized	dejected	delicate

deluded	demanding	demeaned	demented
demoralized	dependent	depleted	depraved
depressed	deprived	deserted	deserving of pain
deserving punishment	desolate	despair	despairing
desperate	despicable	despised	destroyed
destructive	detached	detest	detestable
detested	devalued	devastated	deviant
devoid	diagnosed	dictated to	different
difficult	directionless	dirty	disabled
disagreeable	disappointed	disappointing	disapproved of
disbelieved	discarded	disconnected	discontent
discouraged	discriminated	disdain	disdainful
disempowered	disenfranchised	disenchanted	disgraced
disgruntled	disgust	disheartened	dishonest
dishonorable	disillusioned	dislike	disliked
dismal	dismayed	disorganized	disoriented
disowned	displeased	disregarded	disrespected
dissatisfied	distant	distracted	distraught
distressed	disturbed	dizzy	dominated

doomed	double-crossed	doubted	doubtful
down	down and out	down in the dumps	downhearted
downtrodden	drained	dramatic	dread
dreadful	dreary	dropped	drunk
dumb	dumped	dumped on	duped
edgy	egocentric	egotistic	egotistical
elusive	emancipated	emasculated	embarrassed
emotional	emotionless	emotionally bankrupt	empty
encumbered	endangered	enmity	enraged
enslaved	entangled	envious	estranged
evaded	evasive	evicted	excessive
excluded	exhausted	exploited	exposed
fake	false	fatigued	fear
fearful	fed up	flawed	forced
forgetful	forgettable	forgotten	forlorn
fragile	freaked out	frightened	frigid
frustrated	furious	futile	gloomy
glum	gothic	grey	grief
grim	gross	grossed-out	grotesque

grouchy	grounded	grumpy	guilt-tripped
guilty	harassed	hard	hard-hearted
harmed	hassled	hate	hateful
hatred	haunted	heartbroken	heartless
heavy-hearted	helpless	hesitant	hideous
hindered	hopeless	horrible	horrified
horror	hostile	hot-tempered	humiliated
hung up	hung over	hurried	hurt
hysterical	idiotic	ignorant	ignored
ill	ill-tempered	imbalanced	impatient
imposed-upon	impotent	imprisoned	impulsive
in the dumps	in the way	inactive	inadequate
incapable	incommunicative	incompetent	incompatible
incomplete	incorrect	indecisive	indifferent
indignant	indoctrinated	inebriated	ineffective
ineffectual	inefficient	inferior	infuriated
inhibited	inhumane	injured	injustice
insane	insecure	insignificant	insincere
insufficient	insulted	intense	interrogated

interrupted	intimidated	intoxicated	invalidated
invisible	irrational	irritable	irritated
isolated	jaded	jealous	jerked around
joyless	judged	kept apart	kept away
kept in	kept out	kept quiet	labeled
laughable	laughed at	lazy	leaned on
lectured to	left out	let down	lethargic
lied about	lied to	limited	listless
little	lonely	lonesome	longing
lost	lousy	loveless	low
mad	made fun of	man handled	manipulated
masochistic	messed with	messed up	messy
miffed	miserable	misled	mistaken
mistreated	mistrusted	misunderstood	mixed-up
mocked	molested	moody	nagged
needy	negative	nervous	neurotic
nonconforming	numb	nuts	nutty
objectified	obligated	obsessed	obsessive
obstructed	odd	offended	on display

opposed	oppressed	out of place	out of touch
over-controlled	over-protected	overwhelmed	pain
painful	pain-filled	panic	panicky
paranoid	passive	pathetic	perplexed
pessimistic	petrified	phony	picked on
pissed off	plain	played with	pooped
poor	powerless	pre-judged	preached to
preoccupied	prejudiced	pressured	prosecuted
provoked	psychopathic	psychotic	pulled apart
pulled back	punished	pushed	pushed away
put down	puzzled	quarrelsome	queer
questioned	quiet	rage	raped
rattled	regret	regretful	rejected
reluctant	resented	resentful	resigned
responsible	retarded	revengeful	ridiculed
ridiculous	robbed	rotten	sad
sadistic	sarcastic	scared	scarred
screwed	screwed over	screwed up	self-centered
self-conscious	self-destructive	self-hatred	selfish

sensitive	shocked	shouted at	shy
sick	singled-out	slow	small
smothered	snapped at	spiteful	stereotyped
strange	stressed	stretched	stuck
stupid	submissive	suffering	suffocated
suicidal	sullen	superficial	suppressed
suspicious	tempted	tense	terrified
threatened	timid	tired	torn
trapped	troubled	uncomfortable	unhappy
unimportant	unloved	unmotivated	unpopular
unsure	upset	useless	vengeful
weak	wearied	whacked out	worn-out
worried	worthless	wrong	

QUANTUM SOUL
CLEARING STATEMENTS

"Mother/Father, God/Goddess, Creator; Absolute, Ultimate, Infinite, Radiant-Golden, Quantum Source-Light and I are ONE. We work together as a unified, quantified, co-creative team. By the Power, the Authority and Divinity inherent within me, through my connections with, and Oneness as Absolute, Ultimate, Infinite, Radiant-Golden, Quantum Source-Light, please prep to work, clear and create. Please prepare, place, establish and strengthen Quantum Source-Light containment and protection fields around me and each of my loved ones; our homes, places of work, vehicles, finances, financial interests, gifts, expressions, and intellectual properties. Clear and remove all types of extra souls and entities, dark portals, toxic streams and decaying universes, all their effects and everything they represent from in, on, around and through me and my loved ones. Clear all negative motivations, blocks and interferences, and all blocks to positive expressions, and clear all sparks, programs, issues and challenges that I may be running throughout all times, places and spaces; at all levels layers and depths of my Being."

"Clear _____ (and everything it represents)."

"Clear _____'s need (and everything it represents) to be in my body, my energy bodies, and ME, all my systems; my ego and all its systems; my mitochondria, all their generations and all their systems; all my generations and all of their systems; my proteins, environments, associations and entanglements; my personal and the collective consciousness, sub-consciousness and un-consciousness; all personal, planetary and universal core operating systems; all my interfaces and connections to all those systems; and how it's affecting me in any way, shape or form, time, place or space, at all levels, layers and depths of my Being."

"Clear MY need for _____ (and everything it represents) throughout my body my energy bodies, and ME, all my systems; my ego and all its systems; my mitochondria, all their generations and all their systems; all my generations and all of their systems; my proteins, environments, associations and entanglements; my personal and the collective consciousness, sub-consciousness and un-consciousness; all personal, planetary and universal core operating systems; all my interfaces and connections to all those systems; and how it's affecting me in any way, shape or form, time, place or space, at all levels, layers and depths of my Being."

"Break resonance with _____ (and everything it represents) throughout my body my energy bodies, and ME, all my systems; my ego and all its systems; my mitochondria, all their generations and all their systems; all my generations and all of their systems; my proteins, environments, associations and entanglements; my personal and the collective consciousness, sub-consciousness and un-consciousness; all personal, planetary and universal core operating systems; all my interfaces and connections to all those systems; and how it's affecting me in any way, shape or form, time, place or space, at all levels, layers and depths of my Being."

"Break and clear the habit and/or addiction of _____
(and everything it represents) throughout my body my energy
bodies, and ME, all my systems; my ego and all its systems; my
mitochondria, all their generations and all their systems; all my
generations and all of their systems; my proteins, environments,
associations and entanglements; my personal and the collective
consciousness, sub-consciousness and un-consciousness; all personal,
planetary and universal core operating systems; all my interfaces
and connections to all those systems; and how it's affecting me in
any way, shape or form, time, place or space, at all levels, layers and
depths of my Being."

"Please apply the highest most powerful Quantum Source Light
Clearing statements that will fully and completely clear and remove
_____ (and everything it represents) throughout
my body my energy bodies, and ME, all my systems; my ego and
all its systems; my mitochondria, all their generations and all their
systems; all my generations and all of their systems; my proteins,
environments, associations and entanglements; my personal and the
collective consciousness, sub-consciousness and un-consciousness;
all personal, planetary and universal core operating systems; all my
interfaces and connections to all those systems; and how it's affecting
me in any way, shape or form, time, place or space, at all levels, layers
and depths of my Being."

Forgiveness Statement

I willingly forgive myself for any and all, actual or perceived, hurt
or harm I may have caused myself or any others; or that any others
have caused me or any others with _____ and everything
it represents.

I willingly love and forgive myself.

I willingly love and forgive all others.

All others willingly love and forgive me.

I willingly love and forgive God/Source.

God/Source willingly loves and forgives me.

I willingly love and forgive my Quantum Source-Light Highest Self.

My Quantum Source-Light Highest Self willingly loves and forgives me.

I am absolutely, ultimately, infinitely, quantumly loved and forgiven.

I now willingly release all _____ and everything it represents, and go in peace, love, joy, harmony, health, wealth and abundance

"Clear _____ (and everything it represents) from my body and all its systems. Final clear it now."

"Clear _____ (and everything it represents) from my energy bodies and all its systems. Final clear it now."

"Clear _____ (and everything it represents) from ME and all my systems. Final clear it now."

"Clear _____ (and everything it represents) from my ego and all its systems. Final clear it now."

"Clear _____ (and everything it represents) from my mitochondria, all their generations and all their systems. Final Clear it now."

"Clear _____ (and everything it represents) from all of my generations and all their systems. Final clear it now."

"Clear _____ (and everything it represents) from all of my proteins, environments, associations, and entanglements, all their systems, and all my interfaces and connections to all those systems. Final clear it now.

"Clear _____ (and everything it represents) from my personal and the collective consciousness, sub-consciousness and un-consciousness, and all my interfaces and connections to all those systems. Final clear it now.

"Clear _____ (and everything it represents) from all personal, planetary and universal core operating systems, all systems within those systems, and all my interfaces and connections to all those systems. Final clear it now.

"Then clear, transform, flash-burn, purify and sterilize _____ (and everything it represents). Purify it back to source and/or sources; then purify source and/or sources."

The Download

Once the clearing statements above are completed, say the following:

"Please download _____ and everything it represents." (Ask for whatever frequencies you'd like to have the old stuff replaced with—it can be as many things as you'd like.)

Once you've finished your list of things you want to download; then say:

"Please download any other Quantum Source Light frequencies that may not have been said but that are needed in any and all languages."

"Please download, infuse, implement and integrate all these new frequencies and everything they represent. Clear and Remove all old limiting patterns and programs; and replace with all of these New Frequencies and everything they represent at all levels, layers and depths of my Being."

Wait to feel the shifting of the energies then say:

"Activate, Synchronize, Harmonize and Optimize all of these new frequencies and everything they represent. Please integrate and anchor them in at all levels, layers and depths of my Being. Then, please apply them all as functional skill sets."

THE FORGIVENESS STATEMENT

- *I willingly forgive myself for any and all, actual or perceived, hurt or harm I may have caused myself or any others; or that any others have caused me or any others with this _____.*
- *I willingly love and forgive myself.*
- *I willingly love and forgive all others.*
- *All others willingly love and forgive me.*
- *I willingly love and forgive God/Source.*
- *God/Source willingly loves and forgives me.*
- *I willingly love and forgive my Quantum Source-Light Highest Self.*
- *My Quantum Source-Light Highest Self willingly loves and forgives me.*
- *I am absolutely, ultimately, infinitely, quantumly loved and forgiven.*
- *I now willingly release all of this _____ and everything it represents, and go in peace, love, joy, harmony, abundance, health and wealth.*

Forgiveness is a misunderstood practice for most people in the world. Forgiveness is not condoning harmful behavior, nor is it allowing others—or ourselves—to continue to emotionally, mentally, physically or spiritual abuse us. Many times we must physically withdraw ourselves from situations or relationships in order to stop the abusive, painful behaviors.

Forgiveness is the willingness to define what we have perceived or experienced as harmful, and to acknowledge we may have had some type of roll in that exchange of energy at some level and not seek any type of retribution. This ultimately frees us, emotionally, mentally, spiritually and physically. (Remember, we are multi-dimensional beings. This life that we are currently living is a tiny fraction of what we are actually living as a Soul-Being.)

Secondly, we are also acknowledging that others have their role to play in the situation—either as the person being harmed or the person causing the harm. Forgiveness is not about blame and shame. It is about freedom.

Forgiveness is drawing that energetic line in the sand and saying, "I acknowledge that there has been some type of harm or negative engagement. I no longer want to continue in this energetic exchange. By allowing me to withdraw all my energy from you and allowing you to withdraw all your energy from me, we will then no longer have a negative interaction and we can each begin a healing process. I take back my part of this exchange. You take back your part of the exchange. God/Source takes back Its/His/Her part in this whole exchange. My Highest Self takes back it's part of the exchange. The negative charge between us is now resolved and we can free to easily go our own separate ways in peace and harmony."

When said in its entirety and with a willingness and intent to release the energetic binds that cause pain, this statement can clear and void vows, contracts, commitments, etc., that a person has made in all life-times and existences. It can help clear out generational vows (i.e., the tribal vows that perpetuate conflict between groups of peoples in war-torn areas of the world, as well as personal grievances, vendettas and vows we have made ourselves.) And it can help clear out any energies we may be holding for others, that are not ours to hold onto.

These statements allow us to take back our personal power, release victimization, and regain mastery over all aspects of our lives and existences. It energetically allows us to feel forgiveness that we may have been denied by others, causing self-punishment. The statements make/allow us to be responsible for our part in any given situation and it makes/allows others to be responsible for their own stuff, as well. By releasing perceived hurt and harm and applying forgiveness, we release the energetic hold others have had on us and that we've allow ourselves to maintain.

If we, indeed, are God/Goddess Spark—that Divine Core Spark that resides within each of us—and the whole world is our "stage," then we have the power, through our words and our intent to change the landscape of our "stage." We can find and create peace within so that we no longer attract to us the same energies, events, people, etc., that cause us continued pain. As Masters, we have the responsibility to ourselves, our families and our communities to model peace from within, to continue to forgive ourselves and others, and lead peace-filled lives so that others can then learn how to live peacefully. The Journey begins with (and within) us, as individuals, and spreads outwards throughout the world.

RECOMMENDED READING

I want to share with you some of my favorite authors and books that have helped me change my life. Many of these authors, with their works and revolutionary discoveries, have contributed indirectly to the Quantum Soul Clearing Process work *because* of the cutting-edge information and ideas contained in their work.

I continue to grow and evolve, as I know you will, too. As you read these authors, you will gain greater insight into yourself, the world and universe we live in. The more information you have, the greater your ability to expand your mind, your experiences and live more fully.

This is by no means a complete list! I didn't list any of the medical text books I've read, because they are not easy reads! However, I would encourage you to explore biology, anatomy and physiology texts in order to gain a deeper awareness of how the human body really works.

Also, there are several books by many of the authors that are listed below, which I didn't mention specifically, because the list would be longer than it already is!

I suggest that as you read some of these authors, based on your personal interests, you may want to delve more deeply into their works in order to support your own personal path of evolution and enlightenment. I just wanted to give you a sample of some of the people who have impacted my life.

The Dark Side of the Light Chasers, by Debbie Ford

The 21 Day Consciousness Cleanse, by Debbie Ford

The Right Questions: Ten Essential Questions to Guide You to an Extraordinary Life, by Debbie Ford

Resurrecting the Body, Reinventing the Soul: How to Create a New You, by Deepak Chopra

The Ultimate Happiness Prescription: Seven Keys to Joy and Enlightenment, by Deepak Chopra

The Celestine Prophecy, by James Redfield

The Tenth Insight, by James Redfield

Taking the Quantum Leap: The New Physics for Non-Scientists, by Fred Alan Wolf

Dr Quantum's Little Book of Big Ideas: Where Science Meets Spirit, by Fred Alan Wolf

The Biology of Belief: Unleashing the Power of Consciousness, Matter and Miracles, by Bruce H. Lipton

Spontaneous Evolution: Our Positive Future and a Way to Get There from Here, by Bruce H. Lipton

Way of the Peaceful Warrior: A Book that Changes Lives, by Dan Millman

The Power of Now, by Eckhart Tolle

A New Earth, by Eckhart Tolle

The Four Agreements (A Practical Guide to Personal Freedom), by Don Miguel Ruiz and Janet Mills

The Fifth Agreement (A Practical Guide to Personal Freedom), by Don Miguel Ruiz and Janet Mills

The Five Love Languages: The Secret to Love that Lasts, by Gary Chapman

The Field, by Lynne McTaggart

The Intention Experiment, by Lynne McTaggart

Jonathon Livingston Seagull, by Richard Bach

Illusions: The Adventures of a Reluctant Messiah, by Richard Bach

One, by Richard Bach

Conversations with God, Books 1, 2, and 3, by Neale Donald Walsch

The Law of Attraction, by Esther and Jerry Hicks

Ask and It is Given: Learning to Manifest Your Desires, by Esther and Jerry Hicks

The Divine Matrix: Bridging Time, Space, Miracles and Beliefs, by Gregg Braden

The Spontaneous Healing of Belief: Shattering the Paradigm of False Limits, by Gregg Braden

Healing Hands of Light: A Guide to Healing Through the Human Energy Field, by Barbara Brennen

Energy Medicine: Balancing Your Body's Energies and Optimal Health, Joy and Vitality, by Donna Eden and David Feinstein

Frequency: The Power of Personal Vibration, by Penney Peirce

Theta Healing: Introducing and Extraordinary Energy Healing Modality, by Vianna Stibal

Feelings Buried Alive Never Die, by Karol K. Truman

Your Body Speaks Your Mind: Decoding the Emotional, Psychological and Spiritual Messages that Underlies Illness, by Deb Shapiro

Your Body Believes Every Words You Say: The Language of the Body-Mind Connection, by Barbara Hoberman Levine

Heal Your Body A-Z: The Mental Causes for Physical Illness and the Way to Overcome Them, by Louise Hay

You Can Heal Your Life, by Louise Hay and Joan Perrin Falquet

Love, Medicine and Miracles: Lessons Learned about Self-Healing from a Surgeon's Experience with Exceptional Patients, by Bernie Siegel

101 Exercises for the Soul: Simple Practices for a Healthy Body, Mind and Spirit, by Bernie Siegel

Minding the Body, Mending the Mind, by Joan Borysenko

The Power of the Mind to Heal, by Joan Borysenko

Power vs. Force: The Hidden Determinants of Human Behavior, by David R. Hawkins, M.D., Ph.D.

Transcending the Levels and Consciousness, by David R. Hawkins, M.D., Ph.D.

Sidelights on Relativity, by Albert Einstein

The World As I See It, by Albert Einstein

Quantum Physics for Dummies, by Steven Holzner

What the Bleep Do We Know?, DVD

Sacred Contracts, by Carolyn Myss

Anatomy of the Spirit, by Carolyn Myss